Gutenberg

Gutenberg

Stephan Füssel
Translated by Peter Lewis

Published in 2019 by
HAUS PUBLISHING LTD
4 Cinnamon Row
London SW11 3TW
www.hauspublishing.com

Originally published under the title *Johannes Gutenberg*
in the series rowohlts monographien

A CIP catalogue record for this book is available from the British Library

ISBN: 978-1-912208-67-8
eISBN: 978-1-912208-68-5

Typeset in Garamond by MacGuru Ltd

Printed in Czech Republic

Contents

Foreword

Johannes Gutenberg occupies a quite out-standing position in the global history of the media, since it was he who, by combining and further developing a series of technological innovations, succeeded for the first time in reproducing texts in theoretically unlimited numbers and hence in putting knowledge and education at the disposal of everyone.

Gutenberg is therefore the father of mass communication as well as the progenitor of book printing and the print media as a whole and of the dissemination of both scientific knowledge as well as new intellectual and philosophical insights – a process that continues to the present day. At the same time he was a master craftsman in the art of typography, layout and printing and was one of only very few people in the history of technology to have created a masterpiece with the very first thing he ever produced, namely the Bible that bears his name. Gutenberg brought together a multitude of technical developments, ranging from the casting of individual type characters through the technique of type-setting and inking to the actual printing of texts, combining them to such a degree of perfection that it became possible for the first time to disseminate knowledge in a typographical form that was suitably beautiful and in large print runs.

The 18th-century German physicist Georg Christoph Lichtenberg quite rightly remarked in an aphorism that 'the lead in typecases has done more to change the world than the lead in bullets'. And so it was that, as the year AD 2000 approached, Gutenberg was chosen by an American research team as the 'man of the millennium', on the grounds that all significant developments in the centuries that followed, be it Columbus's voyages of discovery, Luther's Protestant Reformation or the Enlightenment in the 18th century, would not have been possible without the effects of the new mass medium of the printed word that Gutenberg had established.

While at the outset Gutenberg directed his publications at the great patron of all the sciences and arts of the Middle Ages, namely the Christian Church, it was the intellectual trend of humanism, with its belief in the general educability of all people, that appropriated this new technological advancement and used it to make available both the key texts of classical antiquity and their translations into the vernacular in high-volume print runs. In addition, the newspaper and the magazine, the handbill and the pamphlet all provided news and background information, creating in the process the phenomenon of public opinion and a forum for the reformation of both the Church and society at large. The weighty folios of the medieval period were supplanted by handy pocket books, while the verse epics of the Middle Ages gave way to the new art of novel writing. Although Latin continued for several centuries to be the language of scholars, by the end of the 16th century, the vernacular had already attained a clear pre-eminence. For almost 350 years, Gutenberg's technological innovations remained unchallenged; it was only the industrialisation and mechanisation of the 19th century that formed the basis for a quantitative expansion of the printing sector. The digital revolution of the present has now largely superseded hot-metal printing and is also in the process of making paper obsolete – and yet the communication revolution instigated by Gutenberg continues unabated.

This monograph combines key facts about the life and times of its subject with an in-depth portrait of the inventor and merchant Johannes Gutenberg, highlighting his position within the history of technology and the history of ideas and, above all, tracing the impact of his revolutionary invention down the ages.

Historical background: the woodcut and the manuscript

'On whatever day you look upon the face of St Christopher, on that day shall you surely not die an evil death.' This legend, carved in Latin beneath one of the earliest preserved one-sheet woodcuts, dating from 1423, illustrates the significance of this saint's image in a very striking way: the image of St Christopher, a much-loved figure in expressions of popular piety who, in religious teaching, could be both a symbol for the omnipotence of God and for practical acts of charity, was widespread thanks to the protection it was believed to offer against the so-called *mors repentina* or *mors mala*, the fear of a sudden or bad death that provided no further opportunity to a person for contrition, repentance and conversion. Even today many depictions of St Christopher can be found in stained-glass church windows, on frescoes and at wayside shrines throughout southern Germany, Austria and the South Tyrol region of northern Italy. The possibility of securing St Christopher's blessing for oneself not just when visiting public spaces or religious buildings but being able to take a saint's image such as this home, is evidence of a first, important change of medium. Hitherto, religious instruction had been confined – alongside the sermon – to the centuries-old tradition of the visual portrayal of biblical and theological subject matter in church windows, on bronze doors, in the sculptural decoration found in places of worship or in mural cycles and panel paintings. The first fundamental change in this state of affairs became apparent at the start of the 15th century, when the Chancellor of the University of Paris, Jean Gerson (1363–1429), who worked tirelessly for the reform of religious life, made the suggestion that 'instructional panels should be hung in churches in order to direct people's ignorance of religious matters'. The Renaissance humanist philosopher and theologian Nicholas of Cusa (1401–1464) was one who took up this suggestion in the German-speaking areas of Europe. In the course of his consultations in German dioceses he had discovered that even the most important prayers were completely unknown to the faithful and priests alike. As a consequence he had a number of 'Our Father panels' installed in various churches.

The single-sheet print of St Christopher was impressed on paper using a woodblock: a preliminary drawing was sketched in reverse on to a block of wood and then all the non-printing surfaces were gouged out with a chisel; the remaining surfaces were inked, and a moistened piece of paper placed on top and rubbed all over with a heavy ball of cloth. During the process the ink would usually soak through the paper, meaning that as a rule the reverse side was not printed on. The visual image and the accompanying text were carved out of a single woodblock, which could be reused several hundred times.

At the beginning of the 15th century, throughout the whole of central Europe, all the basic prerequisites can be found for a mass dissemination of images and texts – namely the availability of paper and the high-pressure technique of woodcut printing.

Paper had been invented in China as early as the 2nd century AD. It first became widespread throughout Asia, but by the 10th century had found its way to Damascus and Baghdad along the Silk Road, and thence, via North Africa with the expansion of Islam, reached Spain and Italy, where the first paper mills in the West were established in the 12th and 13th centuries. By the 14th century paper mills were also operating in France, as well as in Germany from 1390 at the latest when there is clear documentary evidence of a mill run by

St Christopher, coloured single-sheet woodcut, dated 1423, after the copy held in the John Rylands Library, Manchester

one Ulman Stromer in Nuremberg. Even in this early period of its distribution, paper only cost one-quarter of the price of parchment, the costly skin of animals such as calves and kids. The raw material for paper was provided by rags and tatters (scraps of waste textiles), which were soaked and softened in vats before being felted. This raw material was skimmed off sheet by sheet using a sieving frame; wire motifs inserted into these sieving frames ensured that the paper became a little thinner at the point where it touched them, thus allowing this so-called 'watermark' of the motif to show through. Many undated prints can be dated and their precise local provenance determined by means of these watermarks.

The technique of woodcut printing had likewise already been known for many centuries in the Far East. In China, Korea and Japan both the original woodblocks and the resulting impressions on paper of Confucian and Buddhist tenets of faith (Sutras), dating from the 7th and 8th centuries, have survived.[1] Where the incision of texts into woodblocks in this part of the world was concerned, it was primarily about preservation of the ideas rather than mass dissemination. In Korea there are to this day numerous libraries that preserve the woodblocks from which individual prints can be run off. The technique of woodblock printing soon spread to central Asia and reached Baghdad and Cairo in around the 11th century. In the city of Tabriz (modern Iran), under Mongol rule in the 13th century paper money was printed with Chinese characters; some examples of this currency found their way to Central Europe in the 15th century. The advance of the Mongols may also have been responsible for introducing both playing cards and the knowledge of woodblock printing to Europe. By the 15th century, playing cards had become the most popular uses to which woodblock printing was put, together with pictures of saints and items of news on pamphlets.

When a number of single-sheet prints are put together to form a small book, it is referred to as a 'block-book'.[2] The images and texts in such block-books were all carved into wood for printing. We know of certain shorter religious texts that appeared in this form, such as the Ten Commandments or the Song of Songs but also secular practical guides, such as a book on palmistry. One particularly widespread genre concerned the *Ars moriendi*, 'The Art of Dying'. The illustration on page 8 shows one page of illustration and one of text from a German-language manual on dying from around 1470. The text is addressed both to the person facing death and to his companions. The ups and downs of the struggle with death, the temptations

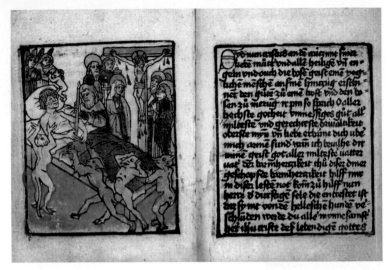

Ars moriendi, block-book c. 1470; a manual on how to die a good death, in the German vernacular

of the Devil and redemption through Christ are conveyed in highly expressive illustrations and short texts.

In parallel with the introduction of the technique of woodcut illustration, over the course of the 15th century the production of manuscripts freed itself from the ecclesiastical and monastic realm and began to be practised in secular scribes' workshops. Records indicate that a workshop of this kind, run by Diebold Lauber at Hagenau in Alsace, had been producing and stockpiling religious and secular manuscripts in great numbers since the 1430s; these were illustrated in-house and then sold commercially. Thus, even by the first half of the century, the subject matter, production techniques and the methods of sale and distribution of books had changed fundamentally.

One driving force behind this was the blossoming of the sciences, which prompted a fundamental reform of higher education and the foundation of many universities, such as those in Rome (La Sapienza,

A Korean movable typeset
form and the resulting
printed poem in Hangul
script, 1447

1303), Prague (1348), Cologne (1388), Leipzig (1409), Louvain (1425) and Barcelona (1450). The decisive intellectual tendency of the time was humanism, with its belief in the universal educability of man and in a new intellectual openness, which sought to combine Plato's philosophy with Christianity.

During the 15th century cities grew in importance as a result of the emergence of more simple manufacturing industries, such as cloth and linen production, or innovative proto-industries that worked with wind and water power. Alongside these developments, new forms of financial institutions and banking operations – originating in Italy – were put to the test more widely. The old privileges of the Hanseatic League disappeared, and new trade routes arose that forged close bonds between southern Germany and Italy and France.

Early European university foundations

Prague 1348 – Florence 1349 – Vienna 1365 – St Andrews 1411 – Bordeaux 1441 – Glasgow 1451 – Venice 1470 – Mainz 1477 – Aberdeen 1495

Metal type printing in Korea 1377

Knowledge of Far Eastern printing methods may possibly have come to Europe along such trade routes, although a link of this kind has not been conclusively proven despite intensive research. Experiments using clay stamps for individual characters had been taking place in China since the 11th century, and in Korea with characters cast from bronze and other metal alloys from the 14th century. The year 1377 is indisputably the date of the earliest text printed using movable metal type: the *Anthology of Great Buddhist Priests' Zen Teachings* (the original title is usually abbreviated to *Jikji*) from the Heungdeok Temple at Cheongju in Korea, which has been in the possession of the Bibliothèque Nationale in Paris since 1943. In 2001, alongside the Gutenberg Bible, the *Jikji* was named a 'milestone in the cultural history of humanity' by the UNESCO Memory of the World Programme. Although the huge number of more than

10,000 separate characters in Korean initially proved an impediment to the practical application of the technique of casting and setting metal type, the introduction of the Hangul alphabet by King Sejong the Great (albeit only in 1444!) made it possible to combine new methods of casting with the advantages of a limited set of type characters (see page 9). At first, the casting process was done in sand moulds, which meant that the slugs were unable to retain the same kind of sharpness of edge that was later evident in Gutenberg's technique. However, it is worth pointing out the interesting phenomenon that, almost simultaneously at opposite ends of the known world at that time, experiments were being conducted with very similar technologies. Yet the concentration of Gutenberg's various inventions – from the casting of individual letters, the printing ink and the form of typesetting through to the press itself – was what gave his technique of printing its quite unique character. Another key factor that characterised his technology was the distinct way in which it impacted on the contemporary world, enjoying as it did a largely free development, initially untrammelled by any regulations imposed by the Church, society or trade guilds.

Mainz – Strasbourg – Mainz

The 15th century was a time of new economic and intellectual openness, yet at the same time it was characterised by stagnation in both secular and ecclesiastical politics. The emperor and the rulers of the German principalities – chief among them the electoral princes – were at loggerheads. At the irregularly convened Imperial Diets, the emperor's dependence upon the princes became evident in the Hussite Rebellion of 1419–34 and later in the wars against the Ottoman Turks. The power of the territorial lords increased, and even the cities were frequently accorded a special legal status.

At the beginning of the 15th century the Rhineland city of Mainz had some 6,000 inhabitants, who, in this difficult period of upheaval, formulated and passed a new council constitution giving far greater weight to the right of the city's trade guilds to information and co-determination and reducing the influence of the old patrician families. In the clashes that ensued between the patrician class and the guilds, members of aristocratic families were forced to flee the city on several occasions and also left of their own accord in protest. In the 1540s the city's financial situation became so catastrophic that it was obliged to run up serious debts with the cities of the surrounding region, notably Frankfurt am Main. By 1456 Mainz was to all intents and purposes bankrupt and fell forfeit, so to speak, to its chief creditor and neighbour Frankfurt.[3] Yet during this period Mainz was still able to consider itself a free city; however, following the Diocesan Feud there in 1462 it became an episcopalian and

The oldest known cityscape of Mainz, from Johann Stöffler's *Der römische Kalender*, printed in 1518 by Jakob Köbel in Oppenheim (reversed reproduction); pictured in the foreground is the Fish Gate (Fischtor), behind which can be seen the Cathedral of St Martin and the lower slopes of the Jakobsberg along with the ruins of the old city walls

electoral city. In around 1450 its parlous economic state had led to a recession and a marked drop in population. For this reason, immigration was encouraged, with newly arrived citizens being exempted from all taxes and levies for a period of ten years. Where crafts and commerce were concerned, the city was noted for its timber trade and woodworking industries, shipping concerns, viticulture and agriculture as well as cloth weaving, iron- and non-ferrous metalworking and goldsmithery.

We do not have a definite date of birth for Gutenberg, but, given that a document from 1420 relating to a disputed inheritance indicates that he was of the age of majority by that time, arguments have been advanced putting his birth date at somewhere between 1393 and 1404. In 1900, by international consensus, the turn of the century (1400) was settled on as his symbolic birth date.[4] During Gutenberg's lifetime it was not uncommon to name a child after the saint on whose feast day it was born. Accordingly, 24 June (the Feast of St John) is repeatedly cited as Johannes Gutenberg's birthday. A fair degree of probability speaks in favour of this, even though the name Johannes (also Johann, with the variants Henchen, Hengin or Henne also common in Mainz) was so popular and widespread that we cannot necessarily assume a connection with the saint's feast day. Johannes's father Friedrich ('Friele' in the Mainz dialect) Gensfleisch zur Laden, who was born in around 1350 and who became a citizen of Mainz in 1372, had been married to Else Wirich, his second wife, since 1386. As a patrician in Mainz he was engaged in commerce – presumably in the cloth trade – was a member of the minting house cooperative and was also on several occasions the city's official mathematician. The father did not bear the soubriquet 'zum Gutenberg'; this additional name was only used by members of the family from the 1520s onwards. Since the early 14th century the family had owned the Gutenberg manor house, which was situated at the corner of Schustergasse and Christophstraße in Mainz but which no longer exists. This Gothic building of two storeys provided living space for a number of families and, in all likelihood, also for Johannes's typesetting and printing workshop.

We know nothing of Gutenberg's youth; in view of his good knowledge of Latin and his skill in both the technical and commercial realms most commentators have assumed that he received an education befitting his social status, first at a monastery school and then at university. He may perhaps have attended the St Victor monastery in the south of the city, close to the suburb of Weisenau, learning Latin and the rudiments of science there. The fact that he demonstrably remained a member of the Brotherhood of St Victor into his old age may be an indication that he had, indeed, once been schooled at this institution. Henchen Gutenberg must surely have been forced to leave Mainz when he was still very young, in the company of his father and siblings, since things came to a head once again in August 1411 in the ongoing clash between the patrician

The Gutenberg coat of arms

families and the guilds; this conflict led to an exodus from Mainz of 117 patricians, who hoped thereby to safeguard their privileges of exemption from taxes and other duties. In all probability they decamped for a short spell to Eltville, where the Gensfleisch family had inherited from the maternal side of the family a house in Burghofstraße that abutted the town's defensive wall. Just two years later, in 1413, Gutenberg's father was forced to leave Mainz once more after food riots broke out in the city and would surely have been accompanied by his family members on this occasion, too. Yet a good school education was also guaranteed in Eltville, with the 'general school' attached to the Church of St Peter there providing instruction in grammar and rhetoric from Aelius Donatus's *Ars grammatica* and prescribing the study of other Latin writers.

Only three documents have survived from the first three decades of Gutenberg's life: in the summer semester of 1418 and the winter semester of 1418–19, a certain 'Johannes de Alta villa' was matriculated at the University of Erfurt, which belonged to the Archdiocese of Mainz.[5] It was customary at that time for a person to add their place of origin to their forename, and since several forebears and close relatives owned property in Eltville and the Mainz Gensfleisch family had been compelled to leave Mainz a number of times because of the clashes with the guilds, it is highly plausible that Gutenberg might have styled himself thus. Furthermore, the names of some of Gutenberg's later confederates also appear in this matriculation book: Konrad Humery, who subsequently became one of his business

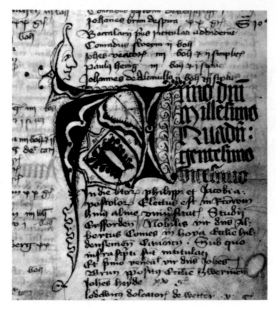

Detail from the matriculation book of the University of Erfurt for the winter semester of 1418–19, with the entry 'Johannes de Alta villa' in the line immediately above the decorative initial letter

partners in Mainz, was matriculated in 1421, while in 1444 and 1448 we find entries for 'Petrus Ginsheym', that is, Gutenberg's erstwhile apprentice and later successor Peter Schöffer from Gernsheim. In the winter semester of 1419–20 Johannes de Alta villa was awarded a bachelor's degree in Erfurt. It was possible to sit this first exam after just three semesters' study according to the curriculum of the faculty of arts, where the seven liberal arts were taught, namely grammar, rhetoric, dialectics, astronomy, mathematics, arithmetic, and music. This course of study then led on to Latin grammar and literature, Greek and Latin philosophy and what we might nowadays call the natural sciences.

Gutenberg's father Friele Gensfleisch zur Laden died in the autumn of 1419.[6] Not long thereafter we find in the records the first definite mention of Henchen Gutenberg, who, together with his brother Friele and his brother-in-law Clas Vitzthumb, became embroiled in a legal dispute with his stepsister Patze Blashoff, his father's daughter from his first marriage, over the latter's inheritance. Because Johannes Gutenberg appears in this case in his own right, he must have reached the age of majority in around 1420.

We do not know where Gutenberg lived in the 1420s or what he studied or qualified in. His name, along with that of his brother Friele, is recorded on just one occasion, in 1427 or 1428, in a document concerning the transfer of a life annuity.[7] On 16 January 1430 his mother, Else Wirich zu Gutenberg, came to an agreement with the city of Mainz over an annuity of 13 guilders owing to her son Johannes.[8] We may deduce from the fact that his mother was dealing with this money matter on his behalf that he could not have been resident in the city at this time.

Finally, a treaty drawn up in 1430 by the Archbishop of Mainz, Conrad III, which was aimed at reconciling the warring parties within the city,[9] indicates that Johannes Gutenberg, who had been driven out of Mainz in 1428, was now granted unconditional leave to return. This document was drafted with the assistance of the cities of Worms, Speyer and Frankfurt and once more guaranteed the patrician class in Mainz numerous rights, including minting their own coins and access to council seats and other public positions. Various exiles who were now permitted to return without any let or hindrance are mentioned by name, among them 'Henchin zu Gudenberg'.

Merchant and inventor

Even so, at that time Gutenberg evidently had no intention of returning, preferring to stay in the cosmopolitan trading and manufacturing city of Strasbourg on the Upper Rhine. With 25,000 inhabitants, it was among the largest cities in central Europe and had one of the most important cathedral masons' lodges, which in the 1430s was in the process of completing one of two planned towers for the city's minster. Strasbourg was also one of the foremost places for bell-casting and paper manufacture and had thriving trade links to both the south of France and northern Italy as well as to Augsburg, Nuremberg and Prague. The earliest document corroborating Gutenberg's presence in the city is dated 14 March 1434: because the city of Mainz was apparently refusing to pay a sum of 310 guilders that was owing to him as an annuity payment, he had the Mainz town clerk Nikolaus Wörstadt, who was passing through Strasbourg at the time, detained in a debtors' prison. Wörstadt had to swear under oath that the outstanding sum would be forwarded to Gutenberg's cousin Ort Gelthus in Oppenheim.

That done, in an adept diplomatic move and with the agreement of the Strasbourg city council, he personally absolved Wörstadt of all responsibility. The municipal accounts book of Mainz verifies that from 1436 onwards the city did indeed make these payments, including the outstanding interest in arrears.[10] Gutenberg was living at this time outside the gates of Strasbourg in the suburb that took its name from the Benedictine monastery of St Arbogast that

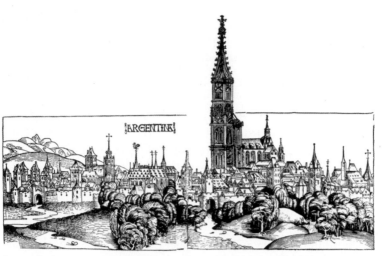

A woodcut engraving of Strasbourg, from the *Weltchronik* of Hartmann Schedel, printed in Nuremberg in 1493 by Anton Koberger

was situated there; he evidently did not acquire citizenship rights, although on several occasions he is mentioned in official documents as being well off and respectable. We only possess an indirect note, which in no way represents any really significant documentation, regarding a complaint lodged against Gutenberg by the Strasbourg patrician lady Ennelin zu der Iserin Thüre, which may perhaps have been about a breach of promise on his part to marry her (*'ut videtur matrimoniae causa'*).[11] This extremely brief note does not entitle us to speculate either on his character or on his marital status over the following decades, and yet it has prompted commentators time and again to fabricate all manner of fantastic interpretations and romantic scenes.

In contrast to this, court records from the year 1439 furnish us with detailed information about his activities in Strasbourg.[12] They show him to be an enterprising merchant, an ingenious inventor and a skilled technician. Accordingly, a Strasbourg citizen by the name of Andreas Dritzehn asked Gutenberg to tutor him in 'a number of skills', so from 1437 onwards he taught him how to 'cut and grind precious stones' – in other words, gave him lessons in the craft of minting and goldsmithery. Together with a group of partners including Dritzehn, Gutenberg also established a finance company to provide start-up capital for a new technical process – a stratagem that would be adopted repeatedly in the years that followed. When Andreas Dritzehn died in 1439 his brothers made a claim for the capital he had invested to be released to them or, failing that, that they should be admitted as partners. The case documents, including a large number of individual witness statements and the verdict of the Great Council of the City of Strasbourg, have been preserved in a facsimile copy.

In addition, from 1438 Gutenberg entered into a contractual agreement with the bailiff Hans Riffe von Lichtenau to produce pilgrimage souvenirs for the next 'relic viewing' in Aachen (Aix-la-Chapelle). Their aim was to manufacture pilgrimage mirrors as mementoes of the journey. Such objects were commonplace in popular religious devotion; pilgrims used them in the hope of capturing in their reflection some of the blessed light that was thought to radiate from religious relics and carrying it home with them. These popular mirrors were made from an alloy of lead and tin and produced in large quantities. The Strasbourg council's verdict of 12 December 1439 in the case of Andreas Dritzehn's investment indicates that a lead alloy must have been involved, since his money was used, among other things, to purchase lead. Andreas Dritzehn had participated in the consortium of his own volition. One of his fellow partners was Andreas Heilmann, whose brother, the pastor Anton Heilmann, provided a detailed witness statement in which he confirmed that the consortium had been established with the express intention of manufacturing pilgrimage mirrors for the *Ochevart* ('the journey to Aachen'). The only difficulties that arose were with sales, since the next pilgrimage, which was due to take place in 1439, did not, in fact, happen until the following year.

However, those involved had signed a second contract, which brought Gutenberg, Andreas Dritzehn, Andreas Heilmann and Hans Riffe together in a 'corporation and community'. In addition to instructing them in mirror-making, Gutenberg was charged with initiating the rest into 'all the arts and adventures with which he was already familiar or which he might henceforth gain knowledge of in some way'. Just the context of these witness statements, and to an even greater extent a quick glance at contemporary documents, indicates that the frequently used turn of phrase 'arts and adventures' does not refer to thrilling escapades but rather was a guildsman's technical term for adept artisanal skills and bold mercantile ventures. These terms have been shown by parallel contemporary sources to be unequivocally and indelibly associated with the realms of craftsmanship and trade and should not – as still happens even now – be used time and again to try to surround the history of Gutenberg's inventions with an air of mystery. Likewise, the fact that the partners gave an undertaking not to make their inventions known

Relic viewings

Churches regularly and readily put their collections of religious artefacts, or 'relics', on public display. Aachen had been an important place of pilgrimage since the 12th century (Charlemagne, who had ruled from there in the late 8th and early 9th centuries, was canonised in 1165). The four 'great Aachen relics' – a robe belonging to the Virgin Mary, Christ's swaddling clothes, the loincloth Jesus wore when he was crucified and the cloth in which the severed head of the martyred John the Baptist was wrapped – were shown publicly in the city's cathedral from 1250. According to reliable contemporary reports, on the days of 'great plenary indulgence' every July some 15,000 to 20,000 pilgrims would journey to Aachen, coming from as far afield as central Europe, Poland, Hungary and Slovenia. In 1440, when Gutenberg's consortium sold its pilgrimage mirrors as mementoes, Duke Philip the Good of Burgundy and his retinue were among the visitors. Because mass-producing religious souvenirs often exceeded the capacity of local trade guilds, the sale of devotional items here was thrown open to all. However, one stipulation was that they had to be sold directly in person within the city.

publicly for the time being was nothing other than shrewd commercial calculation. Decisive keywords from the case files are the references to a wooden press that a turner by the name of Conrad Saspach had made for the consortium, along with records of the purchase of lead, the preparation of 'forms' that were 'cast' and the testament of the goldsmith Hans Dünne, who received over 100 guilders in payment for fabricating everything 'which had to do with printing'. It is perfectly conceivable that the mention of 'forms' is a reference to so-called *literae formatae*, individual letters that were cast in metal. The experiments with a lead alloy and the commission to build a wooden press indicate that these were the first steps in the development of the book-printing process. One of the partners, Andreas Heilmann, owned a paper mill jointly with his brother Nikolaus outside the city gates of Strasbourg. It would have been a logical and plausible step to develop a paper press into a printing press.

A further impetus may have come from the industry of bell founding, which was practised in Strasbourg: individual foundry moulds were used to cast blessings and dates of manufacture into the lower part of the rim of the bell body. The bells were cast in bronze, which contained between 20 and 25 per cent tin. However, it was not just for lettering on bells that stamps of individual letters were used in the early 15th century; this technique was also employed to impress letters on to covers in the art of bookbinding. And in 1444 news came from Avignon that the Prague silversmith Prokop Waldvogel, who was resident there, had devised an *ars scribendi artificialiter*, an 'artificial/skilled method of writing', which in all likelihood referred to a typesetting process using individual die stamps. In Strasbourg Gutenberg was clearly able to profit from the technical experiences amassed by related crafts; the nature of his business connections indicates that, alongside his skill as an inventor, he also possessed outstanding commercial acumen and that he succeeded time and again in enthusing financial backers for his schemes, which involved major investment.

His business partners in Strasbourg either occupied senior and the very highest positions in the city's hierarchy or were eminent merchants and master craftsmen. Hans Friedel von Seckingen, who was responsible for financing and who appeared as a witness in the lawsuit records, loaned Gutenberg considerable sums of money on at least two occasions.[13] The Seckingen family owned the most important commercial enterprise in Strasbourg in the first half of the 15th century. As early as 1400 they had been involved in the metals sector, providing funding for a new method of producing metal scabbards as well as being wholesale dealers in strip brass. In addition, they were involved in long-distance and general wholesale trade and conducted financial transactions with such places as Venice, Milan, Basle as well as Nuremberg and Frankfurt. Furthermore, they had an interest in a German–Lombard trading company and in the central Strasbourg commercial warehouse on the River Ill, which lay at an important intersection of European trade routes. Friedel von Seckingen constantly kept a keen eye on innovative technological developments; for instance, in 1440 he was involved in the construction of one of the first windmills in southern Germany.

During this period Gutenberg evidently developed a rational process for the mass production of pilgrimage mirrors and, in the process, experimented both with alloys of lead and tin and with a model casting. There is also mention of other projects about which, however, the sources do not give any further information. His career as a businessman seems to have gone well, for in 1441 Johannes Gutenberg was accepted by the chapter of St Thomas's Monastery in Strasbourg as guarantor for the sum of 100 livres lent to one Johann Karle the Elder. The following year he borrowed 80 livres from the same chapter, with the well-known Strasbourg cloth merchant Martin Prechter in turn standing surety for him for this loan. According to the figures given in the accounts books, he paid interest on this sum annually from 1444 to 1457. There is also a list of taxes, dating from the time of the Armagnac Wars (1443–4), in

JEAN FUST OU FAUSTE
Associé de Jean Gutemberg Inventeur de l'Art de
l'Imprimerie en la Ville de Mayence vers l'an 1450.

L. Boudan f.

which Gutenberg's property was rated at between 400 and 800 livres and taxed accordingly; the sum levied obliged him to pay half the cost of keeping a horse ready for war service in the defence of the town. In the same context, on 20 January 1444 he was listed as one of the citizens of Strasbourg capable of bearing arms and was designated an 'associate' (in other words, not a full member) of the Guild of Goldsmiths.

In 1444 the wood-turner Conrad Saspach, who had made a printing press for Gutenberg in 1436, left the city of Strasbourg. For the years 1444 to 1448 we have no records indicating where Gutenberg was living; certainly not in Frankfurt in any event, as in August 1447 he appointed a Frankfurt citizen to act on his behalf in the Imperial Court of Justice there to seize the assets of a debtor. Only on 17 October 1448 is there documentary evidence of his reappearance in Mainz. On that date he took out a loan of 150 florins from his relative Arnold Gelthus at a 5 per cent rate of interest. Gutenberg undertook to pay back seven and a half florins in interest annually and subsequently to repay the entire sum. Clearly, as he had done before in Strasbourg, in Mainz, too, Gutenberg needed financially strong partners who were prepared to furnish him with the capital for his experiments, for the development costs of new technical equipment and for the associated labour costs. The fact that considerably larger sums were now required for this enterprise is indicated by his business partnership with Johannes Fust, who in 1449 lent him 800 guilders at a rate of 6 per cent and advanced him a further 800 guilders in 1453 in order to finance their joint 'Work of the Books'. When one bears in mind that in 1450 a decent town-house could be bought in Mainz for around 500 guilders, it becomes apparent that Gutenberg's capital investment costs ran into the millions in modern terms.

By 1450 his preparations were sufficiently advanced that he was able to begin setting and printing both broadsheets and more extensive works.

The new art

Gutenberg's invention was as simple as it was ingenious: texts were broken down into their smallest constituent parts, that is the 26 letters of the Latin alphabet. By rearranging the individual letters, a new fully coherent text results each time. Whereas for centuries texts had been duplicated by being either written down in their entirety on to the page or, just as completely, incised into wood (in the case of single-sheet prints and block-books), now only the letters of the alphabet needed to be cut and cast in metal once and were thereafter available time and again to print whatever text one desired. At root, his second idea was also as simple as it was technologically revolutionary: instead of following the practice commonplace for the preceding 700 years in the Far East – namely of transferring the ink by rubbing over the paper – Gutenberg used the physical properties of the spindle press to transfer the ink from where it had been applied on the type material to the moistened paper by means of the high but, above all, even pressure that the press could bring to bear.

A great number of different steps were required to develop this apparently simple and, on the face of it, obvious procedure. Stamps of individual letters, skilfully engraved by a goldsmith, had been around for quite some time; likewise, casting techniques were known from both bell founding and the manufacture of coinage. What was needed now was to test run the whole idea with the individual letters, the casting technique and the press. At the heart of Gutenberg's inventions was the development of a casting instrument that enabled the operator to align the die precisely and to give every slug cast exactly the same external form. The original instrument from the 15th century has not survived; the so-called 'manual casting device' that is pictured nowadays in many textbooks has come down to us in this particular form only from several centuries later, although all the original type slugs that have been preserved, plus the quality of the prints, provide clear indications that a comparable manual casting instrument must have been among Gutenberg's key inventions.

To begin with, a letter was engraved on to the tip of a steel rod. The individual letter appeared there as a back-to-front image in relief (the patrix); the rod was then driven into softer copper with a hammer to produce a non-reversed, sunken impression of the letter (the matrix). This copper mould then formed the die that had to be aligned into the casting device. The casting material (molten typemetal) was poured into the mould, and the end result was a lead character with a raised and once again reversed letter. Because the casting matrix could be used over and over again, it was capable of turning out a theoretically unlimited number of completely uniform and identical type letters. Although we do not know the exact composition of the metal alloy used, it is possible to reconstruct it from later finds, including one that came to light, not insignificantly, from the old town in Mainz.[14] From these discoveries, it has been possible to deduce that

Gutenberg's inventions

- The basic concept of individual cast letters: patrix and matrix
- Lead, tin and antimony alloy for characters
- Instrument for the casting of type
- Typecases
- Composing sticks and a 'form' for the precise alignment (justification) of type and other elements on pages
- Printer's ink (lampblack and resin)
- Hemispherical leather balls for applying ink to type
- Printing press with a sliding carriage, pin holes for perfect alignment of type areas, frames to protect the non-printed surfaces, cover, platen and bar
- Funding concept for businesses
- Distribution system

A manual typecasting
device (reconstruction)

the material used for making characters in the 15th–16th centuries probably consisted of 83 per cent lead, 9 per cent tin, 6 per cent antimony and 1 per cent each of copper and iron. However, the 17th-century samples from Mainz had a lead content of 73 per cent – significantly lower than earlier examples – while the combined percentage of antimony and tin had increased to 25 per cent. This later composition had the advantage that it cooled down very quickly so facilitated a rapid production of type blocks.

The characters now had to be made the exact same depth as all the others so that no one character would sit higher than those around it in a line of type. The individual letters were deposited in a typecase according to the principle of practicability; that is to say, with the letters most frequently used being placed in the middle, directly in front of the compositor. The individual characters were first inserted into a composing stick, in which the separate lines of type could be assembled with appropriate spacing. To achieve this, typesetters used filler material known as 'leading' (blank strips of lead alloy) to even up the spaces between the characters. Composing sticks were at first made from wood, and later from metal. The next step was to compile the individual lines on a galley – some form of stable wooden board – to form either a column of type or a whole page. Then the entire page was laid in a frame known as a 'form'; this meant precisely aligning the type area and if necessary regulating the space between the lines with the aid of more filler material. The type area was inked up using a hemispherical leather ball mounted on a handle and placed in the press. The paper to be printed was dampened so that it would take the ink better and inserted into a hinged cover above the type area, where it was fixed in place with small pins. A frame was dropped over this,

This woodcut, the oldest known image of a printing press, appeared in *La grāt danse macabre des hōmes* ('Dance of Death') printed in the French city of Lyons in 1499 by Matthias Huss

with an aperture in it the same size as the type area so as to mask off the margins of the paper and prevent them from being marked with ink during printing. Then the carriage with the form containing the set type and the cover with paper and frame were both rolled under the plate of the press (the 'platen'), and this was brought down firmly on the paper with a powerful tug on the long handle operating the screw of the press. This 'first printing' was followed by the printing of the reverse side, in which the pricked holes left by the pins affixing the paper when the front was printed were used for perfect alignment so that the type areas corresponded exactly on both sides of the sheet. Sheets of paper of varying sizes were printed (there were as yet no standardised paper sizes), at first only ever one page at a time, although later innovations saw forms containing two, four or eight pages being printed simultaneously, before the reverse side was then printed and the entire sheet folded. The eight or 16 pages were arranged in such a way that after folding they would appear in the correct sequence.

The first printed works were printed only in black type, with all the decorative elements of the text, such as splendid initial letters, coloured column headings, illuminations and also rubrics (letters highlighted in red) being added in later by hand. At first sight, therefore, many early printed works come across as resembling manuscripts, since they were still at this stage embellished by hand.

Der Buchdrücker.

Ich bin geschicket mit der preß
So ich aufftrag den Firniß reß/
So bald mein dienr den bengel zuckt/
So ist ein bogn papyrs gedruckt.
Da durch kombt manche Kunst an tag/
Die man leichtlich bekommen mag.
Vor zeiten hat man die bücher gschribn/
Zu Meintz die Kunst ward erstlich triebn.

The Book Printer, from the *Ständebuch* ('Book of Trades') published in 1568 in Strasbourg by Jost Amman

As a result, none of the surviving 49 Gutenberg Bibles resemble one another, as their rubrics and illuminations were all done differently. Initially, woodcuts were not printed at the same time as the set type, because it proved extremely difficult at the outset to apply pressure on the platen in such a way that the metal of the characters and the wood of the woodcut printed evenly when set together. Accordingly, therefore, in Ulrich Boner's 1461 collection of fables *Der Edelstein* ('The Gemstone'), which was produced at the workshop of Albrecht Pfister in Bamberg (see the illustrations on page 67), the printing of the illustrations and the typesetting were achieved in two separate passes, even though this made considerable demands on the precision of the printing process.

Although it would also have been theoretically possible to make do with two sets of 26 letters, each in upper and lower case, Gutenberg was clearly concerned to transfer the characteristics of good manuscript production as faithfully as he could to the printed word. He therefore adopted the customary manuscript arrangement of text into two columns and took pains to achieve a very regular width of margin by opting for a justified setting. It was for this reason that he engraved and cast a total of 290 different characters: 47 upper-case letters, 63 lower-case letters, 92 characters with abbreviation symbols, 83 combined characters (ligatures), and five forms of comma. The ligatures – such as ff, fl, ll and st – could save a great deal of space on a line, since they were each cast on a single font. Similarly space-saving were the abbreviations that were taken over from Latin manuscripts; these were used for prefixes (pro-, prae-, per- and so on), case endings of Latin nouns (-um, -am, -as) or for double letters (mm, nn). If taken together with the various lower-case letters, therefore, these enabled a skilled typesetter to set a very well-spaced line. At the same time it is clear that considerable demands were made upon the setter's knowledge of Latin. In order to ensure that the Gutenberg Bible could be typeset simultaneously by a number of compositors, some 100,000 characters had to be cast. This made it possible

for Gutenberg to mimic the manuscript form in all its details while surpassing it in accuracy. The fact that the abbreviations used only make sense in Latin makes it clear that the type used to produce the 42-line Gutenberg Bible (B 42) was initially developed for Latin texts.

The book printing press was made of wood (even during his time in Strasbourg Gutenberg had commissioned a turner to construct a wooden press for him); this was a further development of the spindle press that was used, among other applications, to manufacture paper.

Gutenberg's original inventions also include printer's ink, a mixture of organic materials such as lacquers, oils and resins to which he added lampblack, tar and varnish or similar carbon compounds as colour substrates.[15] There are also trace elements of metals in printer's

Reconstruction of a mechanical printing press from the time of Gutenberg

ink, primarily lead and copper but also titanium, iron, nickel and zinc. X-ray fluorescence analysis can determine the precise proportions of these elements and the results used to ascertain the age of unattributed prints and even the printers' workshops in which they were produced. These new investigative techniques proved to be of invaluable help in answering many unresolved questions in research into incunabula – who, for instance, printed the B 36?[16]

The Gutenberg Bible (B 42) of 1454

Gutenberg's early prints can be divided into two main groups: the minor printings (such as letters of indulgence, calendars and dictionaries) and his master work of 1,282 pages – the Latin Bible. As a model for this latter work, Gutenberg opted for the so-called 'Vulgate' (literally meaning 'things commonly accepted'), that is, St Jerome's late-4th-century translation of the Septuagint. The version of the Vulgate that Gutenberg used was a textual variant, originating in the Rhineland, of a widespread 13th-century Parisian recension (critical revision).

Although the precise manuscript he used has never been found (ultimately, after the printing process was over, it failed to find its way back to its home library, having either been discarded as being of no further use or destroyed or misplaced at some later date), theologians and philologists have been able to identify at least two manuscripts still held in Mainz that are thought to be close to the copy used for setting. One of these is Manuscript Hs II 67 from the Mainz Scientific Public Library (*Wissenschaftliche Stadtbibliothek*), an octavo volume from around 1300 written in an extremely small but very accurate Gothic book hand. This manuscript contains the complete Old and New Testaments in the Paris arrangement, and critical studies of the text verify that large portions correspond closely to Gutenberg's first printing. Above all, there are a large number of special variant readings that the manuscript and the printed Bible have in common.

Another octavo Bible on vellum from the second half of the 13th century, originally from the Jesuit College in Mainz but now likewise in the holdings of the Scientific Public Library (Hs I 381), provides numerous variant readings that point to a Parisian provenance and that reoccur in the Gutenberg Bible. It is noteworthy that, in the case of both of these possible textual models for Gutenberg, we are dealing with octavo editions of the Bible written in a small hand in very densely packed lines. This might explain, for example, the handful of incorrect endings to abbreviations and other small mis-spellings in the typeset text.

A third work that might have served as a formal model for Gutenberg is an imposing two-volume Bible in folio format. It was transcribed from 4 April 1452 to 9 July 1453 – in other words at around the same time as the genesis of the Gutenberg Bible – and its external form, namely the arrangement of the text in two columns, the font used, the rubrication and so on, corresponds very closely to Gutenberg's printed Bible (see illustration opposite). Although the scribe's annotation does not name the place where this manuscript was produced and its Gothic Missal script also displays some differ-ences to the letter forms of Gutenberg's Textura font, this work can nonetheless be taken as an example of the kind of prestigious Bible that existed in the same chronological context. We know for sure that this two-volume Bible was in the possession of Mainz Cathedral in 1566, was plundered from there during the Thirty Years' War, was then owned by the Saxe-Weimar family for 300 years and was finally donated to the Library of Congress in Washington, DC.[17]

Johannes Gutenberg imitated the handwritten version of the Bible in every aspect: he adopted not only the arrangement of the text into two columns, the justified setting (which he was able to further refine in the typeset version) and the way the columns were spaced on the page, which he found to be ideally proportioned, but also the large Missal font known as Textura. This resulted in a very closed setting, since the vertical strokes of the individual letters are

Bible manuscript from Mainz, written in 1452–3 and now in the holdings of the Library of Congress, Washington, DC

pronounced, lending the completed page of type the lattice-like appearance of the warp and weft of a piece of woven fabric (*textura* means 'woven' in Latin).

Johann Koelhoff the Younger's *Kölnische Chronik* ('Cologne Chronicle') of 1499 contains the following account of Gutenberg's Bible: 'Anno Domini MCCCCL [1450] was a golden year, for this was when printing began, and the first book that was produced in this way, the Bible in Latin, was printed in a large typeface, which is now used for missals.'[18]

The 'Cologne Chronicle' therefore not only placed the inception of the art of book printing in the solemn context of a sacred year but also located it within the tradition of liturgical texts. The Missal letters that Gutenberg employed were written comparatively large in the manuscripts (and also subsequently in the printed texts) so that they could be read without difficulty by worshippers during services in gloomy church interiors. Given this relatively large font size, the extensive text of the Bible required a double folio format (307 × 445 millimetres) and occupied 1,282 pages. In order to make optimal use of the paper, Gutenberg experimented with the number of lines per column. In his first attempt at setting the text he began with 40 lines per column (on sheets one to five and 129 to 132), while on the verso of sheet five he increased the number to 41 lines per column before settling, from sheet six on, on 42 lines per column throughout. Later, in what is demonstrably a new setting, he began straight away with 42 lines. Examples of both variations in setting can still be seen today.[19]

In the first setting Gutenberg also tried to replicate the work of the rubricators and so printed sheets one, four and five as well as 129 and 130 with additional red type. Thereafter, however, he gave up printing in red and did not even attempt to repeat the experiment on the corresponding sheets of the second typesetting run. Since the need to apply the ink twice over and the difficulty in achieving a perfectly

Page from the Göttingen vellum copy of Gutenberg's 42-line Bible (B 42), vol. 2, fol. 235 verso

Decorative lettering from the Göttingen
Gutenberg Bible: left, vol. 1, fol. 231
verso; right: vol. 1, fol. 84 recto

aligned impression evidently caused considerable delays in the work
process, and because the end result was aesthetically unsatisfactory,
he followed the practice of the manuscript era and left all subsequent
rubrication to the professional rubricators. The copies of the B 42 in

Vienna and Munich still contain the complete '*tabula rubricarum*', including precise instructions concerning the exact points at which highlighting of letters in red is to be executed.[20]

In the copy of the Gutenberg Bible printed on paper that is held by the Bibliothèque Nationale in Paris the final sheet of each of the two volumes contains a handwritten note indicating that Heinrich Cremer, a cleric at the collegiate Church of St Stephan in Mainz, was responsible for rubricating, illuminating and binding the two volumes, by the 15 and the 24 August respectively. Thus we have a definite date by which the books must have been completed.

By undertaking a detailed textual analysis and tracing individual abbreviation tendencies, scholars have been able to ascertain that four different typesetters were involved at the beginning of the Bible printing, while, by the end of the process, six setters were involved.[21] These figures were subsequently confirmed by an electron spectrographic analysis of the inks.[22] The casting of the 60,000 or so individual characters needed would have accounted for six months, while the work of typesetting itself would have taken around two years. To produce the finished text, in addition to the setters, at least twelve printers working on six presses would have been required along with other assistants to ink up the print area, feed the sheets into the press and so on. The task of printing 180 copies of the 1,282 pages of text would have necessitated no fewer than 230,760 separate operations on the presses, or a minimum of 330 working days. Because, as a result of the large number of religious feast days, there were only around 200 working days available every year, and since only four presses were engaged on the job at the outset, and also because teething troubles had to be factored in, the time purely spent printing the work must surely have exceeded two years. Prior to this a scribe would have taken three years to copy a single complete Bible, while now over the same period 180 copies could be produced, with around 40 of these being printed on parchment (vellum) and 140 on paper. It cost some 450 Rhine guilders to buy the imported paper for this job, the great majority of which was sourced from northern Italy (most probably from a Piedmontese paper mill), while the vellum, which took 3,200 animal skins to manufacture (each of the 40 copies using 80 skins apiece) cost 200 guilders.

Gutenberg could not possibly have borne this considerable outlay – which did not even include development costs – all on his own. Instead, as he had already done in Strasbourg, immediately after his return to Mainz he set about securing financially powerful partners for his technologically innovative and commercially extremely bold venture. He immediately raised credit to the tune of 150 guilders from his relative Arnold Gelthus and in 1449 and 1452 took out two separate loans with Johannes Fust.

Fust and Gutenberg

The commercial partnership – and its break-up – between Gutenberg and the qualified goldsmith and Mainz businessman Johannes Fust (*c.* 1400–1466) has over the past centuries given rise, on repeated occasions, to far-fetched speculations and one-sided apportioning of blame – until, that is, the legal historian Hans-Michael Empell[23] subjected the sole surviving document, the so-called 'Notarial Instrument' drafted by the public notary Ulrich Helmasperger[24] on 6 November 1455, to a forensic analysis. Empell concluded that this document provided clear evidence that it was Fust who was pressing for the partnership to be dissolved once its initial purpose, namely completion of the 'Work of the Books' (that is, the Bible printing), had been achieved. This proposed dissolution evidently created a number of financial 'winding-up problems' relating to the sum to be repaid, possible interest accruing and to potential counterclaims on the part of Johannes Gutenberg.[25]

Alongside the documents from Strasbourg, the Notarial Instrument is one of the most important records of Gutenberg's life and the impact of his work and so warrants a fresh examination on account of the objective statements it contains. According to this document, Fust's first loan to Gutenberg, in 1449, was of 800 guilders and was accompanied by a written agreement to successfully complete a joint enterprise that was already under way. Gutenberg wanted to use the loan to produce the tools he needed and at the same time mortgaged them to Fust. In return for this line of credit,

The Helmasperger
Notarial Instrument, 1455
(detail showing the mark
of the notary's office)

Gutenberg was required to pay the customary interest of 6 per cent. Three years later Fust placed another 800 guilders at Gutenberg's disposal, although this time (according to the latter) not in the form of credit but as a capital investment in the joint business venture. Fust, he claimed, had given him a verbal assurance that he would not demand any interest in return for advancing him this money, and in addition maintained that the sum had not been paid in full. Furthermore, Gutenberg went on, he had also invested his own money, for instance, in ensuring the welfare of his colleagues who should, by rights, have been paid by Fust.

The court now pronounced an even-handed judgement. If Fust could prove that he had himself incurred interest in raising the credit then he would also be entitled to demand this from Gutenberg (this ruling related to the first tranche of 800 guilders). On the other hand, Gutenberg was granted leave to demonstrate by way of an invoice the extent to which he had provided funds out of his own pocket. The court clearly based its decision on the assumption that both submissions were true and that justice could be done for both plaintiffs.

Gutenberg did not appear at the court hearing; his representatives were his printers Berthold Ruppel (Bechtolff von Hanauwe) and Heinrich Keffer as well as the former priest of St Christoph, Heinrich Gunther. Fust was accompanied by his brother Jacob Fust and the typesetter and printer Peter Schöffer. Certain details of the case are fascinating – one example being the fact that Fust had taken on responsibility for meeting the costs of parchment, paper and printer's ink as an investment in the joint project. The court ruled that Fust was entitled to repayment of the first loan of 800 guilders and that he had also proved his case where the question of interest was concerned; Gutenberg, however, was granted the right to claim his own costs against the second tranche of 800 guilders.

Of particular importance is the critical reappraisal that this court case was not the reason why Fust and Gutenberg parted company but rather that Fust's decision to continue printing using his own workshop and to dissolve the partnership with Gutenberg was clearly taken immediately after completion of the Latin Bibles – that is, in 1454 – and that this legal dispute only served to clarify the terms on which their partnership was to be wound up. There are no objectively proven indications to suggest that Gutenberg might not have been in a position to meet Fust's demand for repayment. The letter written by Enea Silvio Piccolomini (see pages 44 and 145) largely confirms that the Bible printing was complete by 1454, while a handwritten entry in a vellum copy of the B 42, which up to 1945 was kept in the German Book and Manuscript Museum of the German National Library in Leipzig and which is today in the holdings of the Russian State Library in Moscow, even indicates that this task was already over by 1453.[26]

The two business partners parted company and evidently went on to print separately in their own workshops. Among other things, Gutenberg continued his work on the Donatus and Kalender (or DK) type, some isolated examples of which he may even have produced in Mainz in 1452. He may possibly also have developed a new Gotico-Antiqua type (a half-Gothic, half-Roman typeface) in which the *Catholicon* was set in around 1460 (see pages 70–74). Commentators have often taken the fact that, from 1458 onwards, Gutenberg was no longer paying the interest that he still owed to St Thomas's Monastery in Strasbourg as evidence that he was in financial difficulties. Yet, because there are no other documents to hand on this subject, this argument should be treated with caution. In 1474, after Gutenberg's death in other words, the sum was finally written off as unpaid in the monastery's accounts book.

Fust may perhaps have had a portion of the Bible edition that was at his disposal completed to his own specifications (cf. the copy that is now in Burgos, Spain, illustrated on page 48) and printed with his publisher's mark. In addition, he set up an independent printing operation with Peter Schöffer developing among other things a new typeface, Psalter type (see pages 85–90).

A key witness: Enea Silvio Piccolomini
In this context, an extremely valuable letter should be introduced into the discussion. On 12 March 1455, Enea Silvio Piccolomini (1405–1464), the secretary and imperial counsellor of Emperor Frederick III (1415–1493), wrote to the papal legate Cardinal Juan de Carvajal (1400–1469) to tell him about a momentous encounter he had had on the occasion of the Frankfurt Imperial Diet, which had sat from 15 to 28 October 1454. Piccolomini reported that he had met there a 'marvellous man' (*vir mirabilis*), who had presented astonished onlookers with quinternions (sections of five folded sheets containing 10 leaves or 20 printed pages) of a Latin Bible 'executed in a very neat and legible script', which they were able to read without the

slightest trouble and 'without the use of glasses'. Soon after, some of these quinternions had also apparently been sent to the emperor in Wiener Neustadt.

Piccolomini said that he had heard from several witnesses that 158, or perhaps even 180, copies had been printed. He reported that he would have dearly loved to purchase one for Cardinal Carvajal, but he discovered that 'there was already an ample sufficiency of buyers lined up [...] even before the volumes came off the press'.

This source tells us that Gutenberg, Fust or Schöffer was quite aggressive in touting their printed sheets at the Frankfurt Book Fair, which for many centuries had been a marketplace for manuscripts, and that while there they chanced upon one of the leading humanists of the age (and the future Pope Pius II, 1458–1464), who paved the way for the introduction of book printing in Italy, first at St Scholastica's Abbey in Subiaco and then in 1467 in Rome. Yet the fact that printed material was also sent directly to Emperor Frederick III in Wiener Neustadt demonstrates how this forceful marketing approach reached the upper echelons of not only the Church but also the state.

In addition, this letter proves that Gutenberg's edition of the Bible sold out very quickly and hence that sufficient revenue flowed back to Mainz. We do not know for sure whether subsequent payments were made to the business partners Gutenberg and Fust, nor whether they were paid by subscription, down payment, payment of the balance on delivery and so on. However, by the time the Helmasperger Notarial Instrument was drawn up on 6 November 1455, it is possible that Gutenberg and Fust were sharing the profit and loss of their joint enterprise. Yet publication of the first significant book in the history of printing also witnessed the end of the successful business model of a collaboration between an inventor and a financial backer, and – insofar as we can reconstruct the circumstances – both printing workshops were henceforth to be regarded as separate entities. But before discussing the subsequent development of the technology, we should examine in greater detail the printing of the Bible and another example of outstanding illumination.

To date, 49 copies of Gutenberg's 42-line Bible are known to exist; on some of these the illumination and rubrication were clearly arranged by Fust and Schöffer. Each of these copies is unique, since every one of them was individually embellished. The activity of the rubricators consisted primarily of using fine red lines to highlight *nomina sacra* or to emphasise individual upper-case letters. Picking out the beginnings of sentences in this way made the text easier to read. The illuminators would then furnish the printed text with elaborately ornamented initial letters and possibly other embellishments. According to the importance of any particular passage, space was left over two, three, four or even ten lines for the illuminated initial letter. As a result it was possible for buyers of the works to have their copies decorated according to personal, contemporary or regional taste. As with the book illuminations of the High and Late Middle Ages, certain schools of illuminators with regional or period-related peculiarities can be identified in the embellishment of printed texts, a practice which lasted for some 30 to 40 years.

The Burgos Bible

The first page of the second volume of the B 42 from Burgos (illustrated on page 48) shows three handwritten lines in red ink, a large initial letter 'I' set next to the left-hand column and, in the right-hand column, a decorated initial 'P', which is indented into the text over six lines, begins the opening word of the phrase *'Parabolae Salamonis'*, the 'Proverbs of Solomon'. The slim, tapering tail of the more significant letter 'P' fits harmoniously into the centre space between the columns, while the tail of the initial 'I', which curves towards the book's gutter, transforms into a fantastic sinuous curl of foliage richly decorated with gold leaf. The floral elements, which are not naturalistic but are figments of the illuminator's imagination, flow playfully around both columns. In common with the volume as a whole, the colours on this page are well coordinated: light, bright colours, often toned with white, complement one another splendidly. Light green, light blue and various hues of red and beige produce a well-balanced total picture. One striking feature is the two crossed knotted sticks in the middle of the foot of the page, with foliage arabesques growing out of them. These remarkable segments of branches feature in other books – for instance, in the first volume of a Gutenberg Bible that has survived in only fragmentary form and which can be seen today in the Pierpont Morgan Library in New York. Although the foliage of the New York copy forms different shapes and is also coloured differently, the hand of the same book illuminator is unmistakably visible here, not least because of this central

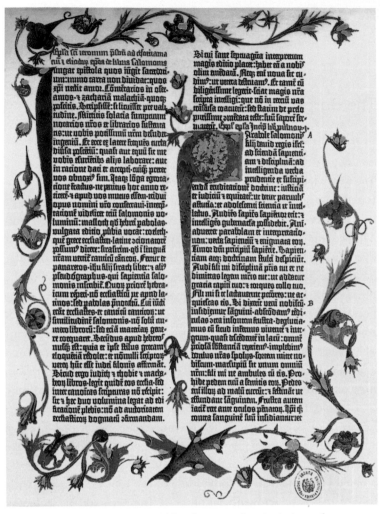

Page from the 42-line Burgos Bible, illuminated at the behest of
Johannes Fust

motif of the crossed knotted sticks. We can also see the same hand
at work in a copy of the 48-line Bible printed by Fust and Schöffer
(1462), in an edition of the collected works of Cicero dating from

Colophon of the *Codex Justinianus*, 1475, with the publisher's mark showing the conjoined escutcheons of Fust and Schöffer

1465, the *Constitutiones* of Pope Clement V (1460), all the illuminated copies of Guillaume Durand's *Rationale divinorum officiorum* (1459) and the 'Decretals' of Pope Boniface VIII (1465). Because all of these works were printed in the Mainz workshop of Fust and Schöffer, and the Latinised surname *Fustis* means 'a gnarled stick' or 'cudgel' in English, the surmise soon arose that these segments of branches were a visual pun on Johannes Fust's name. A final, decisive piece of evidence was provided by the joint publisher's mark found on works produced by the printing partnership of Fust and Schöffer, which shows their separate coats of arms suspended from a knotty stick of this kind.

The Göttingen Model Book

The illumination of one of the extremely rare complete parchment copies of the 42-line Gutenberg Bible, which today is held in the State and University Library at Göttingen, can be traced to another school of book illustration in Mainz and demonstrates that the illuminator who worked on this copy adhered strictly to the patterns set out in a model book. The Göttingen B 42, which is one of just four complete vellum copies in existence worldwide, is uniformly rubricated on each of its 1,282 pages and was decorated by an expert illuminator. The other complete printed copies on vellum can be found in the British Library in London (this copy is thought to have originated from the charterhouse in Mainz), the Library of Congress in Washington, DC, (from the Benedictine monastery of St Blasien in the Black Forest) and the Bibliothèque Nationale in Paris (from the Benedictine monastery of St Jacob in Mainz).

The copy in Göttingen contains handwritten column headings in red Missal script, while the chapter numbers and the beginnings of chapters are written alternately in red and blue.[27] All initials are highlighted and some of them augmented with delicate braiding patterns, while the large initial letters are lavishly embellished with burnished gold and bright colours and attached foliage scrolls (cf. the illustrations on pages 37 and 38). The beginning of the Bible and the first pages of the individual books of the Bible are decorated with trailing foliage depicting acanthus, ferns or briars.

The design elements of this copy consistently follow the templates which appear in a model book from the mid-15th century, which quite by chance has also been preserved in the collection of the Göttingen library (cf. the illustrations on page 52).[28] The model book is extremely interesting, describing in detail as it does not only the illuminators' choice of colour and the painting techniques but also the composition of colours. It begins by setting out coloured patterns for the foliage scrolls and then for the chequers and rhombuses that appear in the background designs. There follow patterns for certain initials and decorative plant elements. The individual stages involved in the execution of foliage and the chequered backgrounds are described in exhaustive detail. The same form of foliage is recommended throughout, with a soft raspberry-red colour on the upper surfaces of the leaves and a deep leaf green on the undersides. Finally, there are descriptions of a light blue and a deep red akin to that of lead oxide, along with a burnished gold with a somewhat powdery appearance. The deep red, the book explains, is obtained from a special species of wood, brazilwood, with the addition of lye, chalk and alum. It is a far brighter colour than the carmine commonly used by illuminators in the High Middle Ages, which is characterised by a heavier corporeality. For the different green tones, mountain green or slate green (also called malachite green) were used as a base, with a sap-green wash on top for shading; this final element was obtained from a plant-based varnish whose composition can no longer be determined with any certainty today. The gold tones were achieved through a mixture of mercury, tin, sal ammoniac and sulphur. The resulting gold colour was more restrained than that of gold dust or gold leaf, both of which were also used for highlighting and contrast. Additional depth and surface effects were achieved by applying spots or short strokes of white lead.

The model book not only describes how to mix colours but also instructs illuminators how to apply them in order to build up a fully finished illustration. A comparison of both the colours and the form of painting clearly reveals that this model book must have formed the

Two templates for book illuminators from the *Göttingen Model Book* (manuscript on vellum, c. 1450); among other works, the copy of the Gutenberg Bible now housed in Göttingen was illuminated according to the patterns prescribed in the model book. Left: fol. 10 verso; right: fol. 8 verso

basis for the illumination of the B 42 from Göttingen. A microscopic photographic analysis has shown beyond all doubt that the composition of colours and their progressive layering in the Göttingen Bible faithfully followed the instructions given in the model book.

The *Göttingen Model Book*, fol. 3 recto; compare the pages of the
Göttingen Bible on pages 37 and 38 illuminated with these same
decorative elements

Large print runs in DK type

One of Fust's grievances against Gutenberg in 1455 was that the latter had not invested funds in their joint 'Work of the Books' but instead had devoted his energies to other projects. And it is true that there exists a whole series of smaller prints, broadsheets, letters of indulgence, brief grammar primers and calendars that we can confidently date as being contemporaneous with the Gutenberg Bible. Intriguingly, these texts are all set in a different type, which it has become customary to refer to – after the types of publications in which it was used – as the 'Donatus and Kalender type', also known as Gutenberg's 'original type'. Again, we are dealing here with a Textura font, albeit one that was heavier and in larger sizes than the type used for the B 42. Here, too, a multitude of abbreviations, ligatures and variants were cast, enabling us to reconstruct a total of 202 separate characters. Following numerous improvements, DK type was used to print the 36-line Bible (*c.* 1458–60, possibly in Bamberg, Bavaria).

Undoubtedly one of the most lucrative undertakings in smaller printed works was the Church's commission to produce a large print run of letters of indulgence. These documents, which were later to become a major focus of controversy and criticism during the Reformation, played a key role in liturgical practice in the 15th century and were by this stage already widespread in handwritten form. Letters of indulgence were issued in return for individually determined monetary donations; at their next confession the bearers could present them to obtain complete absolution from all temporal punishments for their sins. The text of these letters was couched in formulaic terms, and all that was required was for the individual's name, along with a date and signature, to be inserted on the sheet, which was only printed on one side. In this respect, the new potential for mass reproduction offered by the printing process was ideally suited to this enterprise. Just a single side of set type needed to be prepared and then run off in large numbers. In the case of the first two printed letters of indulgence, we know that several editions of each were produced. And in the years that followed there is evidence of print runs numbering in the several thousands. The importance that recipients attached to these letters of indulgence may be gauged from the fact that many of the printed letters that have survived were printed on expensive parchment.

The catalyst for the Church's invitation to tender for printing indulgences was the widespread fear provoked by the continuing advance of the Ottoman Empire. When Sultan Mehmet II captured Constantinople on 29 May 1453 a threat that had thus far seemed somewhat remote suddenly loomed dangerously large. Fear of the 'Turks' – a generalised term encompassing the conquests of the Ottomans and the spread of Islam as a whole – was widespread. As early as 12 April 1451 Pope Nicholas V granted John II, King of Cyprus, the income raised from an indulgence valid for the period from 1 May 1452 to 30 April 1455. From the late summer of 1454 the Cypriot commissary Paulinus Chappe had these letters of indulgence printed in Mainz.[29] The earliest extant example has a handwritten date of 22 October 1454.

It is possible that letters of indulgence had already been produced in Mainz some two years previously, for on 2 May 1452 Nicholas of Cusa granted the prior of St Jacob's monastery authorisation to sell 2,000 indulgences to the citizens of Frankfurt.[30] However, to date not a single copy of this edition has come to light. The example of a letter of indulgence illustrated here (page 56), from the collection of Göttingen University Library, uses as its font a typeface known

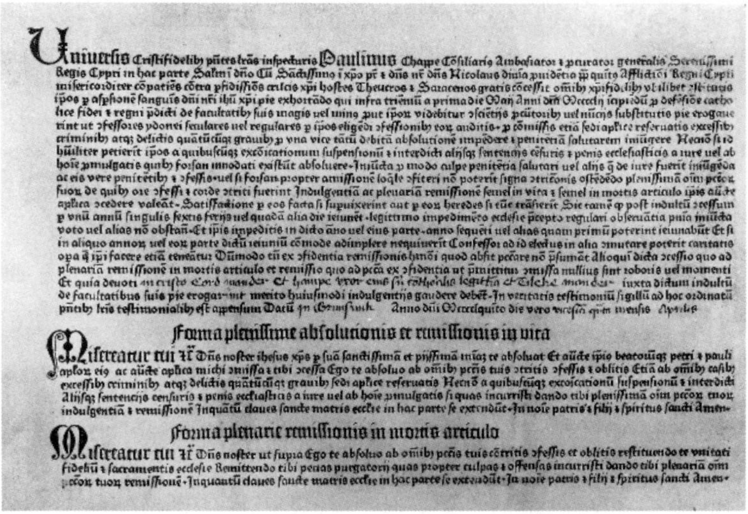

A 31-line letter of indulgence, printed in 1455 on behalf of the Church in Cyprus

as Druckbastarda, a script that was widely employed on official documents in the days of manuscripts. The Donatus and Kalender typeface also appears on this indulgence as a special display font. The copy shown here comes from the fourth edition of this printing, from 1455 (a handwritten note dates it to 26 January of that year), and was printed on vellum.

One of the most active proponents of a crusade against the Turks was the emperor's secretary Enea Silvio Piccolomini, who gave a speech to this effect at the Imperial Diet in Frankfurt am Main on 15 October 1454. As we have seen, printed signatures of Gutenberg's Bible were already in circulation on this occasion. The Diet at Frankfurt also hosted one of the most powerfully eloquent agitators against the 'Turks', the crusade preacher Johannes Capistrano. Given Gutenberg's proximity both in time and space to these events, it should come as no surprise that the first pamphlet printed by his workshop had the Ottoman threat as its subject matter. The publication in question was a calendar for the year 1455, with the title 'A Warning to Christianity Concerning the Turks'. Only one – albeit complete – copy of this small six-page pamphlet has survived and is now in the collection of the Bavarian State Library in Munich (see page 58); it, too, was set in DK type.[31] The verifiable stock of characters in this typeface consists of 93 minuscules (lower-case letters), as well as abbreviations and punctuation marks, but only 15 majuscules (upper-case letters). Because the majuscules K, W, X, Y and Z are lacking, we can assume that this typeface was used for setting Latin texts. In the German-language pamphlet against the Turks, the printers made do by using lower-case letters in place of the missing capitals. A number of worn characters suggest that typesetting materials were kept in use for a long time. The calendar for the year 1455 only contains the dates of the twelve full moons; the primary aim of the work was clearly to act as a rhetorically effective piece of propaganda:

Almighty King enthroned on high,
We pray you henceforth heed our cry:
Let not our heathen Turkish foe
For his misdeeds unpunished go.
Constantinople scarce can bear
The blood of Christians slaughtered there [...]

Over the following twelve months first the Pope, then the Holy Roman Emperor, the crowned heads of Europe, the Kingdom of Germany, the Free Imperial Cities and ultimately the whole of Christendom were exhorted to rise up against the Turks.

Because the pamphlet included news of a communiqué concerning the war against the Ottoman Turks, which was only issued in Frankfurt on 6 December 1454, and the calendar commences on 1 January 1455, we may conclude that it was printed during the second half of December 1454 in Mainz.

The lines of the pamphlet run on continuously in spite of the fact

zu hecuia Die tez hcil;s uõ cõſtãcinopel
was Alſo iſt ym begegclient gar ein grof
ſer has Wñ iſt dr curchẽ uil folkes mdõ
geleget Almechtig got du wolleſt diner
criſtẽheit pleget Wñ gnedeclich gebẽ crafft
fridẽ uñ einikeit Wñ das ſie ſich mit ir
groſſen macht bereitẽ Den ubeln turken
uñ ſin folck zuũtribe Wñ dz ſie ir keinen
lebendig laſſe blybẽ · wedũ in turky gre
tie aſye noch ecopa Dz helff uns die kõ
nigin maria Die do iſt ein mut d heilgẽ
criſtẽheit Der ein ſweer yres miſelidens ir
hertz uſneit Do ir ſon in dotlichem unge
mach Wirwont hãgẽ an dr creutz ſprach
Ich befelen dich dem iungern min Alſo
laß dir die criſtenheit befolen ſin Wñd
bidde gnedeclich vor ſie in aller not Das
dii nuwe am himmel ſtat Off dinſtag
noch nicolai des milden herren Wor mit
tage ſo ſehs ſtunde her zu keren •••:•••••
~~Eyn gut ſelig nuwe Jar~~

'A Warning to Christianity Concerning the Turks', calendar for the year 1455; the closing line reads '*Eyn gut selig nuwe Jar*' ('Best wishes for a very blessed new year').

that the text is written in rhyming couplets. At first sight, therefore, one gets the impression that what we are dealing with here is a piece of prose. The intention of this setting was clearly to save space; furthermore, the text was left ragged, with word breaks at the ends of the lines. The author of the pamphlet is unknown, although the language is sprinkled with Central Rhineland and Alemannic dialect forms. It is thus perfectly possible that the text originated in Strasbourg or the Alsace region and was then typeset by a printer in Mainz. Various attempts to pinpoint the author have so far remained unconvincing.

In a solemnly worded papal bull (*Bulla Turcorum*) of 29 June 1455, the next Pope, Calixtus III, also called upon the whole of Christendom to embark upon a military campaign against the Turks. Christians, he declared, should either join this crusade in person from 1 May 1456 onwards or support it with their prayers and donations. Accordingly, printing of the bull translated into German would have taken place between June 1455 and April 1456. The translator, Bishop Heinrich Kalteisen from Drontheim, who was born in Koblenz, was also responsible for propagation of the Catholic faith throughout the German Empire. He prefaced his work thus: 'Here, in German, is the papal bull and indulgence that our most Holy Father and Master Pope Calixtus sent to us, in opposition to the evil and accursed tyrant the Turks. Anno MCCCCLVI et cetera.'[32]

A copy of this pamphlet of 14 sheets, with 25 printed pages, has been preserved intact in the Berlin State Library, and a facsimile version was produced as early as the beginning of the 20th century. The Latin version of the bull, printed by Gutenberg at the same time as the German translation, is held by the Scheide Library at Princeton in the USA; like the German text, this is the only extant copy.

Judging by the nature of its typography, another Church document that was set and printed in DK type by Gutenberg – the 'Provincial Romanorum' – dates from 1457; this is a gazetteer in Latin of all archbishoprics and bishoprics. In all probability the original printed document comprised ten sheets; although none has been preserved in its entirety, a large fragment of sheets two to nine is today in the holdings of the Library of the Academy of Sciences in Kiev, Ukraine.[33]

To date only a fragment of another early printing by Gutenberg has come to light, in Paris. The sheets in question are the months January to June from a 'Bloodletting and Purgative Calendar' for 1457. The similarly quite imprecise dates of the new moon given here were evidently also calculated by the same author who wrote the 'calendar' warning of the Turkish threat. In accordance with other works of this period that offered medical advice (there are manuscripts of such texts going back to 1439), this text provides information on which days of the month were best for a person to be bled and when it would be most efficacious to take laxatives.

There is also a single-sheet printing dating from this same period;

again, only a fragment has been preserved, in Cambridge University Library. This is a German-language version of a so-called 'Cisiojanus', a mnemonic poem in twelve verses, one for each month, which was designed as an *aide-mémoire* to help the user learn the calendar of liturgical feast days by heart. Its name is derived from the first lines of the Latin original: *Cisio Janus* (a contraction of *circumcisio Januarius*, or 1 January, the Feast of the Circumcision of Christ). Because these mnemonic poems, which had existed in the German vernacular since the 14th century, did not relate to a particular year, this fragment cannot be conclusively dated. However, the worn printed characters point to the second half of the 1450s.

Schoolbooks

In addition to publications produced for ecclesiastical use – the Bible, the letters of indulgence and the pamphlets propagandising against the 'Turks' in both spiritual and secular terms – schoolbooks above all were a genre of text that was attractive to early printing enterprises. In particular, the Latin grammar (*Ars grammatica*) of the late Roman grammarian Aelius Donatus (*c.* 310–380), the teacher of St Jerome, was widely disseminated both as a manuscript and in printed form. His *Ars minor* for beginners was regarded throughout the Middle Ages as the most important primer in this subject, and during the 15th century was printed over one hundred times, while, in addition, some copies appear in the form of block-books, meaning that the entire text was carved into a woodblock from which prints were then run off. Above all, this popular textbook proved to be a valuable cash cow for early German and Dutch printers.[34] During Gutenberg's lifetime, at least 24 editions of Donatus's work were printed in Mainz alone, mostly in his original typeface, which takes the first part of its name – Donatus and Kalender – from this school-book. Despite the large number of copies of this printed work that are still extant, not one complete copy from Gutenberg's workshop or any of his immediate successors has ever been found, with only fragments having been preserved inside bindings and elsewhere. Quite clearly, these schoolbooks were recycled by the schools. Thanks to their comparatively short extent of just 28 pages, they could be set and printed quickly and sold relatively cheaply.

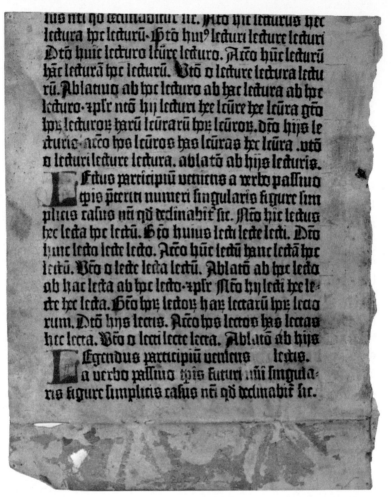

Fragment from the Latin grammar of Aelius Donatus, possibly printed by Gutenberg

However, to teach pupils the five declensions of Latin nouns and the four verb conjugations, no user-friendly instructional aids such as tables or catalogues of the different forms were used; instead, the examples were set in running text. The only elements that broke up the text were the beginnings of the respective chapters, which were highlighted by red initial capitals that occupied a depth of two lines and were added in later by hand. The words given as examples of conjugation are – as is the case right up to the present day – the verbs *legere* and *docere*. All the fragments that have come to light are printed on vellum. This allowed them to be used by a succession of schoolchildren. The surviving 24 editions in the Donatus and Kalender type are subdivided into the 26-, 27-, 28- and 30-line Donatuses. The earliest of these are thought to be the 27-line Donatus fragments, which may possibly date from the early 1450s. The 26-line fragments were printed in the 1460s. Apart from these, there are also editions with the refined DK typeface that was used in the 36-line Bible and which were therefore presumably printed in Bamberg, also in the 1460s.

Editions of Donatus's grammar served as a textbook throughout the whole of the Middle Ages, although it was precisely the advent of book printing, with the revival of the philological sciences and the humanists' reversion to classical, Ciceronian Latin, which ensured that the work was ultimately supplanted in the 16th century, when it was eclipsed by more sophisticated and comprehensive grammars.

In 1901 a fragment was discovered in Wiesbaden of an astronomical calendar showing the position of the planets for the year 1448 and then for 1467 (and so on). The particular configuration of the DK type used demonstrates beyond doubt that this work was produced by Gutenberg after the printing of the *Bulla Turcorum* in 1455 or 1456. A test print of the calendar found in the Jagiellonian Library in Cracow confirms this typographical finding, especially since the reverse of the proof sheet contains a proof of a 40-line Bible using the font of the later 36-line Bible (B 36). This then appears to be a proof dating from the period leading up to the genesis of the B 36, which is believed to have been printed from 1458 onwards. Both fragments indicate that six sheets with the astronomical data must have been glued together, creating a large type area of around 65 × 75 centimetres. This was clearly an early form of poster, on the casting or the interpretation of horoscopes.

The same type material was used to print a broadsheet containing a prayer in Latin entitled '*Respice, domine sancte pater*', which was written by Ekbert von Schönau. A solitary copy of this single-sheet printing, measuring 20.5 × 29.5 centimetres, has survived and is held by the University Library in Munich.

Difficulties in dating arise in the case of a small fragment of the 'Sibyl's Prophesy'. This fragment, which is printed on both sides, displays uneven lines, inconsistent weight of printing of the individual letters and incomplete lines of text. The fact that the edges of the characters are not sharp might lead one to suspect that they had not been cast properly or that experiments had been undertaken with the casting device. Moreover, because the characters were pressed into the paper with varying degrees of firmness, it is reasonable to conclude that the casting of the letters was irregular. And since the fragment is printed on both front and back with continuous text, in all likelihood we are not dealing here with a proof page. Yet any further speculations founder on the sheer brevity of the fragment. The 'Sibyl's Prophesy', which consists of rhyming couplets, originated in the second half of the 14th century and was based on an earlier (late-13th-century) *Sangspruch* – a form of gnomic, single-stanza song. The work was widely known thanks to its religious content and was highly regarded: more than 40 manuscripts from the 14th and 15th centuries are still in existence today. Consequently, there are no grounds for the supposition – raised several times in the research literature – that a contemporary event in the secular world lay behind its publication or explained the particular date it appeared, for new editions of the text kept appearing throughout the late 15th and early 16th centuries and were extremely popular. Because the DK typeface was, as we have already seen, initially cut and cast for Latin texts, the 'Sibyl's Prophecy' cannot possibly have been the oldest known work from Gutenberg's press as has sometimes been suggested. In as much as the poor state of preservation of the fragment even permits an evaluation, the print likely dates from the second half of the 1450s.

We can see that, alongside his principal endeavour on the 'Work of the Books', Gutenberg also typeset and printed a whole series of steady earners – such as schoolbooks, calendars and letters of indulgence – which found their precisely calculated markets. These brought in a regular flow of income, an injection of capital that was badly needed in order to fund the protracted work on the Bible. We can also see that alongside the quality aspect (namely the aspiration in the printed version of the 42-line Bible of not just copying the manuscript but, where possible, surpassing it), the quantity aspect of the new invention also became apparent: heavily used texts such as schoolbooks or letters of indulgence in particular, could, given the minimal amount of typesetting they required, be produced in very high print runs and in a very short time.

The 36-line Bible

As mentioned earlier, the test print of the 'Astronomical Calendar' in Cracow has on its reverse side a proof of a 40-line Bible set in a typeface that is a further development of the DK type. Because a larger point size of the font was used here, however, there was only enough room to print 36 lines per column (illustrated on page 68). The result of this was a marked increase in the extent of this Bible, which, with a total of 1,768 pages, was almost 500 pages longer than the 42-line Bible (B 42). This typeface had only 186 individual characters, and as a result the abbreviations and ligatures could not be applied with the same subtlety as in the B 42. Accordingly, the margin alignment was not adhered to nearly as precisely as in the earlier Bible version. We know from a rubricator's note on a cut sheet in the Bibliothèque Nationale in Paris that the task of rubricating the B 36 was completed by 1461. Printing must therefore have taken place between 1458 and 1460. A philological investigation shows that the text on the first twelve pages follows an unknown manuscript but thereafter consistently adheres to the wording of the B 42. The 36-line Bible is considerably rarer than the B 42, with only 13 complete copies and an additional number of fragments having survived. There are no indications whatsoever of the size of the print run. Since no printer's notes have been preserved in this Bible either, we can only speculate on where it was printed and by whom. Because the setting and printing of the B 36 have also been expertly done, there can be no doubt that a highly experienced typesetter and printer was responsible.

Uns mals ein affe kam gerât·Do er vil guter
nuſſe vant·Der herre er geſſe greene·Jm waſ
gelaget von dem kerne·Der wer gar luſtiglich un=
de gut·Heſuwet was ſein ſhûmer mut·Do er der
pitterkeit empfât·Der ſchale darnach zu hant·Be=
greiff er der ſchale bitterkeit·Von den nuſſen iſt mir
geſeit·Sprach er das iſt mir worden kunt·Si ha=
ben mir verbonet meinen munt·Jhn warff er ſir
zu der ſelben fart·Der kerne dre nuſſe jmmer wart·
Dem ſelben affen ſein gleich·Beide iung arm und
reich·Die durch kurze pitterkeit·Verſchmehet lan=
ge ſuſikeit·wenne man das feuer enzunte wil·So
wirt des rauches dick zu vil·Der thut einem in den
augen we·weil man darzu blieſet mer·Biſz es en=

wie der man·Hat und leſt den iungen gan·ließ er
den knabê reiten·Und lief dem knaben pei der ſeiten

Daran thet er vil palſ·Do der alt erhoret das·Dô
dem eſel ſaſz er do·Der iung ſaſz auff und was fro·
Der ein zu dem andern ſprach·Do er den knaben
reitt ſach·ward getreuer geſelle mer·Der alt mag
wol ein narre ſein·Das er leſt reiten den knaben·
Der ſolt laufen und trabk·Vnd ſolt der alt reiten·
Vil kaum mocht er gepeiten·Das der alt auff den
eſel kam zu dem knaben und reiten hin dan·

Ulrich Boner's collection of
fables *Der Edelstein*, printed in
Bamberg in 1461 by Albrecht
Pfister

Incipit epla sancti Jeronimi pbri
ad paulinu
pbrm. de oib
diuine hysto
rie libris:
Frater am
brosius mi
chi tua munuscula perferens de
tulit simul. et suauissimas litte
ras:que a principio amiciciaz
fidem iam pbate fidei et veteris
amicicie noua preferebant:Ve
ra eni illa necessitudo est. et xpi
glutino copulata. qua non vti
litas rei familiaris. non presen
cia tantu corpoz. non subdola
et palpas adulaco:B dei timor
et diuinaz scripturaz studia co
ciliat. legim9 in veterib; histori
is quosda lustrasse puincias.
nouas adisse ipsos maria tra
sisse:ut eos quos ex libris no
uerant corã qz videret. Sic pita
goras memphiticos vates. sic
plato egiptu et architã tarenti
num eandemqz orã ytalie que quo
dam magna grecia dicebat. la
boriosissime pagrauit. ut qui
athenis mgr erat et potens. cu
iusqz doctrinas achademie gig
nasia psonabat. fieret peregrin9
atqz discipulus malens aliena
verecude discere quã sua impu
denter ingere. Deniqz cu litteras
quasi toto orbe fugiētes psequē
tur. captus a piratis z venunda

tus. tcia tyrãno crudelissio pa
ruit ductus captiuus vinctus
z seru9: Tamē qa philosoph9:
maior emēte se fuit. Ad tytu li
uiu lacteo eloquēcie fonte ma
nãtem. de ultimis hispanie gal
liarũqz finibus quosdã venisse
nobiles legim9. et quos ad co
templacionem sui roma non
traxerat. unius hominis fama p
duxit. Habuit illa etas in audi
tum omnibus seclis celebrãdũqz
miraclm:ut urbem tantã ingsi
si. aliud extra urbem quererent
Appollonius siue ille magus
ut uulgus loquitur siue philo
sophus ut pytagorici tradūt:i
trauit psas. pṫiisuit caucasu
albanos. scitas. massagetas.
opulētissima regna indie peue
niit. z ad extremu latissio philo
amne tñsmisso puenit ad brag
manas : ut hyarcã in throno
sedentē aureo. et de tantali fõte
potantē:inter paucos discipu
los de natura. de morib; de die
rũ ac sydeñu cursu. audiret doce
tem. Inde p elamitas. babiloni
os. chaldeos. medos. assirios.
parthos. syros. phenices. ara
bes. palestinos. reuisus alexan
dria:p rexit ethiopiam:ut gig
nosophistas et famosissimam
solis mensã videret in sabulo :
Inuenit ille vir ubiqz qd disce
ret:z semp pficiēs. semp se me

A page from the 36-line Bible (B 36), probably printed around 1460 in Bamberg

We know for certain that the Bamberg printer Albrecht Pfister worked with precisely this B 36 typeface from 1461 onwards at the latest, and this has repeatedly given rise to the claim that he could also have been the printer of the B 36 itself. However, the fact that Pfister's first known dated printing, namely Ulrich Boner's *Der Edelstein* of 1461, does not display anything like the same quality of typesetting tends to undermine this argument somewhat. Far more convincing, by contrast, is the evidence that every last one of the ten different kinds of paper that were used to print the B 36 came from mills in Bamberg, and that most of the extant copies of this Bible were originally in the possession of monasteries in the Bamberg region. It may then be pertinent to ask whether employees of Gutenberg might perhaps, in around 1458, have taken a complete set of his print materials with them and relocated to Bamberg to found a new printing workshop there, which Albrecht Pfister subsequently joined as an apprentice in 1460. Documentary evidence reveals that Heinrich Keffer, whose name appears on the Helmasperger Notarial Instrument as one of Gutenberg's employees, settled in Nuremberg ten years later (1465), and this has led to recurrent claims that he may, in fact, have been the printer of the B 36. Albrecht Pfister had been a secretary to Prince Georg I of Schaumburg, who in 1459 was appointed Bishop of Bamberg. There is evidence which shows that, over the next ten years, Pfister printed and published primarily German-language texts such as the aforementioned collection of fables *Der Edelstein* (see illustration, page 67) and the early humanist treatise *Der Ackermann aus Böhmen* ('The Ploughman from Bohemia') by Johannes von Tepl, both of which were richly decorated with woodcuts.

The *Catholicon*

Whereas all previous books we have discussed were set either in the typeface of the B 42 or in Gutenberg's Donatus-Kalender typeface, in the *Catholicon* of 1460 we encounter a new font in a smaller point size. It has become customary to refer to this as the Gotico-Antiqua, since it goes back to Italian humanist-influenced models while at the same time displaying certain traditional German features. The highly legible font known as Antiqua, which quickly became widely established, above all in Italy, evolved from the humanist minuscule in handwriting, which, in turn, can be traced back to the Carolingian minuscule script of the 8th century. The majority of scripts known from classical antiquity were passed down through the Antiqua font, with the result that the close affinity to the spirit and ideas of antiquity found its external parallel in the adoption of the humanist script. In the workshop of Fust and Schöffer, another Gotico-Antiqua typeface was used to print Guillaume Durand's *Rationale* in 1459 and the 48-line Bible of 1462. Yet, precisely because Fust and Schöffer used a different Gotico-Antiqua, it is likely that the printing of this *Catholicon* in around 1460 was Gutenberg's work. By this time he had entered into a new business partnership, with the Mainz patrician and scholar Konrad Humery, who was to inherit the printing equipment after Gutenberg's death in 1468.

The *Catholicon* had enjoyed widespread dissemination even in the manuscript era; the Dominican Johannes Balbus de Janua (Genoa)

A page from the *Catholicon* by Johannes Balbus, c. 1460

wrote it in 1286 as an aid for clerics and as a way of promoting understanding of the Latin Bible. It comprises a Latin grammar and a dictionary, which goes beyond simply defining words to provide encyclopaedic information. The title *Catholicon* already indicates that this was a 'comprehensive work'. Despite the small point size of the text and its two-column setting, it still runs to 726 printed pages. Once more, this work placed considerable demands on the degree of learning and the know-how of the typesetters as well as on the skill of the printers and publishers. A colophon to the work confidently offers a paean of praise to the book printer's art and to the city of Mainz:

'With the help of the Most High at whose behest the tongues of infants become eloquent and who often reveals to the lowly what he conceals from the wise, this noble book *Catholicon* has been printed and accomplished without the help of reed, stylus or pen but by the wondrous interplay, proportion and harmony of punches and types in the year of our Lord's incarnation 1460 in the noble city of Mainz, of the renowned German nation, which God's beneficence has seen fit to endow with an exalted clarity of spirit and through such a gift of grace to specially mark out above all other nations on Earth.

'For this, may all praise and honour be given to you, Most Holy Father, together with the Son and the Holy Ghost, Triune but One. O *Catholicon*, broadcast praise of the Church through your publication. Never cease singing the praises at all times of the Blessed Virgin Mary. Let us therefore rejoice and say Hallelujah!'[35]

Unfortunately, this colophon does not reveal the name of the printer but just the place of publication. The theologically well-versed author of the colophon may therefore also have been the publisher or the reviser of the work, who is fully at ease quoting biblical passages from the 'Book of Wisdom' and the Gospels of St Matthew and St Luke. The history of the printing of the *Catholicon* has been the subject of much discussion in recent years, since three variants have been identified, each printed on distinct paper stock. While research

Gutenberg at the printing press; this iron sculpture by Karlheinz Oswald (2000) stands outside the Church of St Christopher in Mainz, where Gutenberg was baptised

into watermarks on the paper suggests a later date for the work (after 1468), the colophon with the year 1460 in Roman numerals would appear to be unequivocal. In any case, according to a sale note, a copy of the *Catholicon* was sold to the monastery at Altenberg in 1465. Moreover, the suggestion that the extensive typesetting of this work was done using solid two-line slugs of cast type remains unresolved: according to Paul Needham (1982) these were used to print this work instead of movable single characters. It will be up to future researchers to determine to what extent this early form of stereotyping was employed and whether these slugs were reused to print more copies at different locations on paper stocks that watermarks indicate were only manufactured at later dates (1469, 1472–4).[36]

Gutenberg's final years

Very few details of Gutenberg's life are documented following the dissolution of his business partnership with Johannes Fust. It is only from a deed of obligation executed by the humanist and lawyer Dr Konrad Humery and dated 26 February 1468 that we learn that at the time of his death (which must have occurred prior to this date) Gutenberg was occupying a printing workshop that belonged to Humery. Archbishop Adolph handed the workshop over to Humery on condition that he run it exclusively within the bounds of the city of Mainz and that, in any future sale of the premises, first refusal to purchase should be given to a citizen of Mainz.[37]

Humery, the son of a wealthy Mainz merchant, studied in Erfurt in 1421 and then, until 1423, in Cologne. In 1427 he moved to Bologna to study law, and in 1432 was awarded a doctorate in canon law there. By 1435 he was living in Mainz and working as a legal advisor to the city authorities; in 1444, when the old city council was toppled, he aligned himself with the guilds and so became chancellor and chief clerk of the newly appointed council. He then found employment in the service of two bishops, Dietrich of Erbach and (from 1459) Diether of Isenburg. During the Diocesan Feud of 1461–2 he supported Diether of Isenburg, and as a result was imprisoned by the victorious archbishop, Adolph of Nassau, in 1462, released the following year and ultimately recompensed for his treatment in 1471. It may have been during his incarceration that he translated Boethius's *Consolatio philosophiae* ('The Consolation of Philosophy'), for in the preface he notes that his aim in translating this work was to bring solace to 'all prisoners'.[38] His translation, however, does scant justice to Boethius's final treatise; he intervenes heavily in the text, both abridging and amplifying, and adds his own glosses within the translation. In effect, ancient philosophy is transmuted into a practical Christian life lesson. In doing so he claimed his intention was to make this text more accessible to 'the uneducated' by couching it in 'their mother tongue [...] for the betterment of their lives and their souls'.

In addition to the interesting connection that it attests between this scholarly patrician and Gutenberg – a subject that still requires further investigation – Humery's document is also of great importance for the numerous details it reveals about Gutenberg's life and work. Since Humery ultimately came into the possession of 'a number of forms, cast letters, utensils, materials and other things pertaining to the business of printing', this would seem to indicate a fully equipped printing workshop in the city of Mainz that Gutenberg clearly ran right up to his death. The Archbishop and Elector Adolph II of Nassau had a strong interest in keeping this workshop within his sphere of influence. He had had cause to recognise its advantages on many occasions and had already conferred honours on Gutenberg because of it.

On 17 January 1465 Archbishop Adolph of Nassau granted Gutenberg a benefice as a 'gentleman of the court' in his household; the deed confirming this refers, in a stock phrase, to the 'distinguished and willing service, which [...] Gutenberg has taken on and performed and shall perform in future'.[39] This benefice entitled him to suitable clothing, 20 bushels of corn and two cartloads of wine per year, which were delivered to him at his home in Mainz. He was also absolved of all other services, obligations and taxes. Through both the records of the printing workshop in Mainz and the papers in Konrad Humery's estate, as well as the deliveries of the benefits-in-kind noted above, we know that Gutenberg did not live out his final

Parade held in Mainz on 25 June 1900 to mark the 500th anniversary of Gutenberg's birth

years at the elector's court in Eltville but stayed living and working in Mainz. Indeed, the supply of provisions to Gutenberg's home appears to have been compensation for the free meals otherwise provided to those noblemen who resided at Eltville. The very formulaic terms in which the deed of appointment is couched does not reveal whether Adolph of Nassau meant to recognise Gutenberg's invention overall with this benefice or whether it obliged Gutenberg to carry out printing commissions for the elector in Mainz or Eltville.

There is no documentary evidence confirming Gutenberg's involvement in establishing an early printing press at Eltville, although several pieces of circumstantial evidence certainly point to this: in 1467 the brothers Heinrich and Nikolaus Bechtermünze printed a Latin lexicon in Eltville that was very much along the lines of the *Catholicon*, which was almost certainly printed by Gutenberg in Mainz in 1460. This *Vocabularius ex quo*, which takes its name from its opening words '*Ex quo* [...]', was a Latin–German

alphabetical dictionary compiled for use in schools, and many manuscripts and early printings of this work have survived.[40] Not only
the *Catholicon* served as a source for this handy lexicon but also a
number of other dictionaries from the 11th to the 14th centuries.
This relatively concise, practical vocabulary for school and university
teaching (many of the definitions are not translated but simply left
in Latin) was evidently a bestseller on a par with Donatus's grammar.
The introduction explains that 'in view of the fact that various dictionaries of this kind are too expensive to buy, especially for poor
students, and in addition are too comprehensive in their coverage
and too opaque in their meaning', a new Latin–German dictionary
was being presented here. And, in the book's colophon, the printers
refer to their work in very similar terms to those found in the
Mainz *Catholicon*: 'This small book was diligently embarked upon
in Eltville by Heinrich Bechtermünze of blessed memory, not with
the help of a stylus or pen but rather by means of a certain new and
ingenious invention, to the glory of God, and finally completed in
the year 1467, on the feast of St Leonard the Confessor – namely the
fourth day of the month of November – by Nikolaus Bechtermünze,
brother of the said Heinrich, and Wiegand Spieß of Orthenburg.'[41]

However, it is not just in the form of the colophon and the genre
of book, namely a schoolbook for the teaching of Latin, that the

The spurious portrait of Gutenberg that
appeared in Henricus Pantaleon's 1568
*Prosopographia heroum atque illustrium
virorum totius Germaniae* ('Prosopography
of Heroes and Other Illustrious Men from
the Whole of Germany'), vol. 2, Basle 1568

Bertel Thorvaldsen: sketch of the Gutenberg statue for the *Gutenberg Monument* in Mainz, 1836

Vocabularius ex quo harks back to the *Catholicon*; the same typeface was also used, although the characters were apparently newly cast, since here their imprint is crisp edged and clear. Gutenberg may have sent the matrices used to cast the type for the *Catholicon* to Eltville as a favour to the print shop there and to his bishop. The *Vocabularius* was clearly very much in demand, as we know of further reprintings from Eltville in 1469, 1472 and 1477.

Thanks to Konrad Humery's deed of obligation we also know that Gutenberg died in February 1468. And, towards the end of the century, a literary memoir published by his relative Adam Gelthus informs us that he was laid to rest in the Franciscan church in Mainz. If his tomb was ever marked by a memorial plaque, then this would have been removed as early as 1577 when the church was taken over by the Jesuits. Finally, in 1742 the building was demolished and replaced by a new Baroque edifice. In turn, this new church went up in flames in 1793 when Mainz was bombarded by the combined armies of the German principalities during its occupation by French forces. Its ruins were levelled at the beginning of the 19th century. In the 1930s the Gutenberg scholar Aloys Ruppel (1882–1977) made an attempt to discover Gutenberg's mortal remains by excavating the former nave area of the church.

Bas-relief panels from the plinth of Thorvaldsen's *Gutenberg Monument*: top, Gutenberg in conversation with Fust; below, Gutenberg checking a proof copy with Schöffer operating the printing press

However, the two bouts of destruction ensured that no inscriptions had survived.

No authentic portrait of Gutenberg is known.[42] We may presume that none ever existed in the first place. The oldest datable image of him is a woodcut from the biographical compendium *Prosopographia heroum atque illustrium virorum totius Germaniae* ('Prosopography of Heroes and Other Illustrious Men from the Whole of Germany') compiled by the Swiss physician Henricus Pantaleon (Basle, 1565).[43] Yet, in this same volume, it is noteworthy that the same woodcut is also used to depict no fewer than four other people. Moreover, in the German edition a quite different portrait to that in the Latin edition appears as the alleged likeness of Gutenberg (see illustration page 78).[44]

A copperplate engraving of 1584 by André Thevet shows a figure who is more of a die-cutter than a book printer, and yet this image of a man with a beard (atypical for a person of Gutenberg's social standing) and a fur-trimmed hat has taken root as the standard image of Gutenberg and it appears ahead of this book's foreword.[45] This engraving formed the basis of a multitude of later portrayals, including a painting from around 1700, which was destroyed by fire in Strasbourg in 1870. The picture on the cover of this book shows a copy of this painting made in 1832 for the Mainz City Library, which is now kept in the Gutenberg Museum.

The image that we have of Gutenberg nowadays has also been shaped by the *Gutenberg Monument* created by the Danish sculptor Bertel Thorvaldsen (1768–1844), which was erected in Mainz in 1837. While Thorvaldsen's work is emblematic of the Romantic glorification of Gutenberg that began in the 19th century and reached its ostentatious high point in the Wilhelmine celebrations marking the year 1900, with pageants, plays and oratorios, the bronze bust cast by the artist Wäinö Aaltonen in Helsinki in 1962 (which is now sited outside the Gutenberg Museum) is a much more sober work,

Gutenberg, Fust and the young Peter Schöffer at the printing press.
Engraving from a drawing by Adolph Menzel, 1840

depicting a person with strong, striking features who radiates an aura
of concentration and pensiveness (see page 137).

Scholarly interest in Gutenberg only began some 200 years after
his invention of the printing press and was instigated by the Dean of
Münster Cathedral, Bernhardt von Mallinckrodt (1591–1644), on
the occasion of the bicentennial of the invention,[46] which at that time
still focused primarily on Fust and Schöffer. In the aftermath of the
next centenary, 1741 saw the publication of the treatise *Hochverdiente
und aus bewährten Urkunden wohl beglaubigte Ehren-Rettung Johann
Guttenbergs* ('A Well-Deserved Rehabilitation of Johann Guttenberg
[*sic*], as Amply Attested in Surviving Documents') by the professor
of history at Göttingen University, Johann David Köhler (1684–
1755), who, as the first scholar to take account of the Helmasperger
Notarial Instrument, laid the foundations for biographical research

Johannes Gutenberg is depicted in romanticised style in this engraving
from an original work by Adolph Menzel, 1840

into Gutenberg. In the 19th century bibliographical listings of incunabula and research into the history of printing and typography
took centre stage. The *festschrift* on Gutenberg that was published in
1900 brought an attestation of the biographical evidence that is still
largely valid today plus a firm attribution of certain printed works to
Gutenberg. The founding of the Gutenberg Society in 1901 and the
Gutenberg-Jahrbuch in 1926 served to significantly promote academic
study in this field. Between 1925 and 1977 research into Gutenberg
was shaped by the museum's director, the city librarian and later
holder of the Gutenberg professorial chair, Aloys Ruppel. In 1939
he wrote what was to be for many years the definitive monograph
on the inventor, which was subsequently consolidated and expanded
by the work of Albert Kapr in the 1980s and Guy Bechtel in the
1990s. The Mainz Institute for Book Studies,[47] founded in 1947, is

now at the forefront of research into Gutenberg, and the findings of researchers are published in the *Gutenberg-Jahrbuch* of the International Gutenberg Society. After many decades in which the focus was on the innovative individual achievement of Gutenberg it is now high time that his advances were viewed within the context of the worldwide development of the media and greater attention paid both to the team of people who invented the printing press and above all to the impact that his work has had down the ages.

The impact of Gutenberg's work

The first successors: Johannes Fust and Peter Schöffer

In a poem accompanying the edition of Justinian's *Institutiones* that was published in 1486 by Peter Schöffer the claim is made in praise of Schöffer that, as an expert in metal-cutting (*sculpendi lege sagetius*), he surpassed 'the two Johanneses'. Following the deaths of Johannes Fust (1466) and Johannes Gutenberg (1468) the high honour of master printer had apparently devolved to Peter Schöffer. A similar opinion was expressed by Abbot Johannes Trithemius in his *Annales Hirsaugiensis* ('The Annals of Hirsau', 1515), in his assertion that Schöffer was responsible for refining the art of typecasting. The first mention in historical records of Peter Schöffer from Gernsheim am Rhein is in 1449, when he is noted as being a copyist and calligrapher at the University of Paris, while, six years later, in the Helmasperger Notarial Instrument, he is identified as 'Peter Girnssheim, scribe to the city and the bishopric of Mainz'. Schöffer and Fust also had a family connection: Schöffer's marriage to Fust's daughter Christine made him the latter's son-in-law.

Because the partnership of Fust and Schöffer always included an imprint and their printer's mark on their printings, their works are easy to identify. They are in all instances masterpieces of the book printer's art, which, with regard to the typographical decorative elements, namely the cutting of dies for the letters and rubrication, carried forward and surpassed the work of Johannes Gutenberg. On 14 August 1457 they produced their first masterpiece, the *Psalterium*

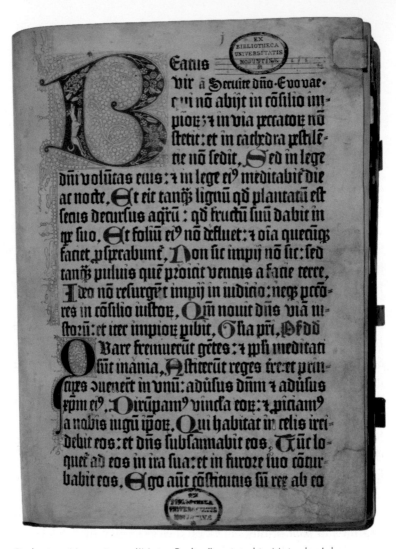

Psalterium Moguntinum ('Mainz Psalter'), printed in Mainz by Johannes Fust and Peter Schöffer, 1457

Moguntinum ('Mainz Psalter') on parchment. For the first time in the history of printing, this work included a colophon and a printer's device. The imprint reads as follows: 'Through the ingenious invention of printing and the formation of letters without any use of a reed pen, this psalter has been designed and executed with all due care to the glory of God by Johannes Fust, citizen of Mainz, and Peter Schöffer from Gernsheim in the year of Our Lord 1457, on the eve of the Assumption of Mary [14 August]'.[48] The new art is designated by the Latin phrase *'ars imprimendi ac caractericandi'*. In ancient usage, *imprimere* denoted an embossing process, thus Suetonius uses this verb to describe a coin or a ring with an image stamped on it. This term, which was transferred to book printing, is reinforced by another verb, *caractericare*. This is nothing but a reiteration of exactly the same process, since *caractericare*, which derives from ancient Greek, means 'to cut into, engrave, carve or stamp', and a 'character' originally denoted a die stamp used to produce coinage and, by extension, came to mean the thing that had been stamped. Whereas *imprimere* signifies the actual printing process, *caractericare* describes the formation of letters or the process of typecasting. The Latin verb *imprimere* has survived in the French noun *imprimerie* ('print shop') and verb *imprimer* as well as in the word 'print' (noun and verb) in English, while 'imprint' is used for the legally enforceable identifying name under which a publisher issues books, and 'imprimatur' (literally 'let it be printed') signifies an official (mostly ecclesiastical) permission to print.

With their 'Psalter', Fust and Schöffer took Gutenberg's basic idea of perfecting handwritten script as far as possible and raised it to a new level of sophistication. Whereas rubrication was only experimented with on a handful of pages in the B 42, in the Psalter rubrication is used systematically for the first time throughout the whole work, while their addition of printed red uncial (a form of majuscule) letters freed them from the need to employ rubricators and their metal-cut ornate initials in red and blue took over the work of the illuminators. The letters in question were kept in three sizes; the illustration on page 86 shows the imposing letter 'B' at the beginning of the first psalm, which measures 8.8 square centimetres and takes up the space of six lines of text in the large typeface in which the book is set. In addition, four-line initials exist for the letters 'C', 'D', 'E' and 'S', together with numerous two-line initials (for example, the initial 'Q' shown on page 86). In each case these are produced from a metal printing block,[49] with the ornamental portion surrounding the initials being engraved into a block the same height as the letter in the manner of a woodcut; once inked up, the block would be placed in the press, and the raised sections would print the design. The printing process would most likely have involved the printer assembling and justifying a complete page of typeset elements, including all the characters and decorative features. Then all the ornamental elements that were to appear in colour would have been removed and inked up separately. The text would then be inked up in black before the whole typecase was reassembled ready for printing. This was undoubtedly a very laborious procedure, but it offered the best way of keeping everything properly aligned and preventing letters from overlapping. A handful of garbled Lombard (Gothic blackletter) initials in the Psalter attest to the fact that these must have got mixed up with the correct type when the complete typecase was reassembled for printing. This first multiple-colour printing in the history of the technology was remarkable in several other ways as well: the font used was a large Psalter type (with a point size of *c.* 39), which consisted of 210 individual characters, and a smaller Psalter typeface (*c.* 32 point) with 185 characters; there were also a total of 53 decorative uncial letters and 228 coloured initials in the three different sizes mentioned. The design of the typeface and the decorative elements, as well as the casting and the setting processes, would undoubtedly have taken quite some time, meaning that the preparations for this printing must surely date back to the years 1453–4, a period when Gutenberg was still active in the print shop they all shared.

All ten extant copies of the Psalter, each consisting of 340 folio pages, are printed on parchment, an indication of the important role they played in the liturgy. The sequence of the psalms, canticles, hymns, antiphons and responses included follows the arrangement in the breviary in use in Mainz, which contained the canonical hours and the songs of the day. That same year saw the publication of a second edition with only 246 pages, which was also permitted to be sold outside the diocese. In 1459 Fust and Schöffer printed a revised edition, the *Psalterium Benedictinum*, which had been reworked according to the guidelines of the Congregation of Benedictines in Bursfeld. The choice of a larger format makes the individual pages appear more harmonious and prestigious. It is possible that this edition was directly commissioned by the Benedictine monastery.

Some of the ten surviving Psalters were originally owned by monasteries in Mainz, for instance, the monastery of St Victor, to which Gutenberg had links, or the monastery of St John. A copy from the Ursuline convent in Hildesheim ended up in the library of Göttingen University, which subsequently presented it as a gift to King George III of England in 1782. It is now in Queen Elizabeth II's private collection in the library at Windsor Castle.

In addition to this Psalter type, the workshop of Fust and Schöffer used a small but easily legible set of Gotico-Antiqua characters for the Latin texts it printed. It was first used for Guillaume Durand's *Rationale divinorum officiorum* (6 October 1459); the same font was also used to set two works of canon law, the *Constitutiones* of Pope Clement V (1460) and the *Liber Sextus* of Pope Boniface VIII (1465).

Another title to emerge from their print shop was an outstanding Bible of 48 lines per page, which was set in a newly cut Gotico-Antiqua font. The use of a smaller point type indicates even at this early stage that these Bibles were intended for personal use rather than for religious services or for reading aloud or teaching. Fust and Schöffer were able to draw on their experience in rubricating the Psalter and as a general rule set all the special display typefaces and the beginnings of chapters and so on in red type. This 48-line Bible (B 48) is among the masterpieces of early printing, with the work now going beyond the realms of direct ecclesiastical teaching and appealing to a wider educated public.

After Johannes Fust's death in Paris in 1466 Peter Schöffer, the husband of Fust's daughter Christine, became the sole heir of both the print shop and the publishing house. From around 1470 he began to include illustrations in his books; in 1484 and 1485, for instance, he published two important and richly illustrated works, the *Herbarius*, and the *Gart der Gesundheit* ('Garden of Health'), the subject matter of which was plants and herbal medicine. Contemporary herbal medicine was able to draw upon the philological work of the humanists, who had edited ancient Latin texts on the topic, including numerous works that had been translated from the Greek. The writings of Theophrastus – a pupil of Aristotle and the father of botany – had only recently been rediscovered and studied. These works, which were compendia of theological, philosophical,

Herbarius, Mainz, Peter Schöffer,
1484

Gart der Gesundheit ('Garden of Health') page showing roses; this example of a popular handbook on herbs was printed by Peter Schöffer in Mainz, 1485

medical, folkloric and natural scientific knowledge and interpretations, convey to us an impression of the healing arts in antiquity.

Schöffer's *Herbarius* was printed in Latin in his Psalter type; as was then customary, no author's name was given. The book was manifestly a compendium of basic instructions about medicinal herbs that was aimed at a broad-interest market. Its 348 pages were illustrated with a total of 150 woodcuts, mostly showing outline sketches of plants; hatching and shading were only rarely used so as to leave plenty of space for colours to be added. The depiction of the plants appears very stiff, suggesting that pressed plants were used as models for the drawings.

The following year Peter Schöffer published *Gart der Gesundheit*, a popular edition of the *Herbarius*, now translated into German. Its 720 pages were illustrated with 378 newly commissioned woodcuts. Unlike the *Herbarius*, this work was not merely a digest of knowledge from antiquity but rather provided an overview of everything that was known about medicinal plants in the 15th century. The first chapter discusses the pharmacological properties not only of plants but also of animals and inorganic materials. The book's second chapter then goes on to provide systematic information about laxatives, aromatic substances, gums and resins, fruits, seeds, tubers, rocks and animals. An index listing 314 illnesses refers the reader in each case to the recommended plant remedy.

The spread of book printing

From the time the first books produced by Gutenberg began to appear up to the year 1500 – which, for purely bibliographical reasons, is defined as the end of the incunabula period – some 30,000 different printed works were published that we can still definitely account for. Assuming a print run of 300 copies per work, this means that at least 9 million books were printed during this period. Over 80 per cent of these were in Latin, the European *lingua franca* for both the Church and secular scholars. Of course, this brought enormous benefits to many print workshops throughout the length and breadth of Europe, since the potential market for their publications was not limited to what, in some cases, were very small language areas. Thus, from a very early date, the Frankfurt Book Fair, for example, developed into a key trading centre for books from France, the Netherlands and Italy. Books were transported there in barrels as untrimmed sheets and, as a rule, only bound into ornately decorated books once sold. While the first books were, by virtue of their intended purpose, still large-format tomes for use in religious services or university libraries, from around 1480 on the format became noticeably smaller. This period also saw the emergence of the title page, which conveyed key information concerning the author, the book's subject matter, its place of publication and its printer. Hitherto, following the tradition observed in manuscripts, these details were included in the colophon at the end of the text. Yet because book production in the print age was no longer geared to individual demand but instead took place in advance with copies being stockpiled for sale, in book depositories it had to be clear at a glance which titles were which. Alongside the change in format and the development of the title page this transitional phase is also characterised by an increasing use of pagination, namely the adoption of page numbers, and the beginnings of book advertising on printed posters.

As reading became ever more widespread we find a growing number of prose versions of Middle High German epics in print, works which had been passed down over the centuries through public recitals in verse form. As a result, this new medium of communication gave rise to a new literary genre, the prose romance, which covered a multitude of diverse works, including travel reports such as *Fortunatus*, satirical cautionary tales like *Till Eulenspiegel*, translations of sagas from the French such as *Melusine* and original narratives like the *Historia von D. Johann Fausten*. Yet publications in the vernacular were not confined to entertaining romances; they also included didactic tracts, herbals and life lessons.

Early German-language publications were produced in Bamberg at the print shop of Albrecht Pfister, who, in 1463, followed his 1461 printing of the fable collection *Der Edelstein* with the most important document of early German humanism, Johannes von Tepl's *Der Ackermann aus Böhmen*. Pfister not only printed works in German he also illustrated them with large-format woodcuts. The first printed work to originate in Bamberg, in around 1459, may well have been the aforementioned B 36.

Roughly contemporaneously with Bamberg, printing was also going on in Strasbourg; as early as 1460 a rubricated copy of the undated 49-line Bible printed in the city by Johannes Mentelin appeared there. Mentelin (*c.* 1410–1478) used his own typefaces, a Gotico-Antiqua font and other pure Antiqua faces. He refrained to a large extent from using initial letters or woodcuts, concentrating instead on producing philologically exact editions of the works of

Hystoria sigismunde/der tochter deß fürsten tan
credi von salernia/vnd deß iünglings gwisgardi·
Oncredus was ain fürst von sa=
lern /gütig vnd ainer senftmütig
en nature· Wo er allain in dem
alter sine hend nicht vermässiget
het mit blütvergiessen zwaie lieb
habenden menschen/der selb hat
all syn lebtage kain kinde ye ge=
hept/daß ain ainige tochter/da im öch vast besser
gewesen wer/oz er dero nit gehept hett· Vnd als
die selb tochter ain ainig kind was· Also hat er
öch sie ainig lieb gegen ir so innerlichen in väter=
licher liebe enzündet/wie wol vil ir zü der ee beger
ten·iedoch wyle er die vngern von im schaide heß
tett er sye über die gebürlichn iare by im haimant
beheben· Doch zeletst als die des hertzogen sune
von Campania vermehelt warde /Ist sie dar nach
bald als der selb ir man gestarb/widerumb haim
zü ierem vater komen·

A page from Niklas von Wyle's translation into German (1476) of
Giovanni Boccaccio's novella *Guiscardo and Sigismunda* from the
Decameron; this is a typical example of the new prose romances that
became popular with the spread of the printed word

the Church Fathers St Augustine of Hippo, Thomas Aquinas and St Jerome. He also printed the writings of Albertus Magnus and the first Bible in German. Other works to emerge from his workshop were the collected works (*Opera*) of the Roman poet Virgil and the comedies of Terence. From the catalogue of manuscripts produced by the scribes' workshop of Diebold Lauber at Hagenau in Alsace, Mentelin also acquired a list of medieval courtly poetry, such as Wolfram von Eschenbach's epic *Parzival* and the fragment *Titurel*, both of which appeared in printed form in 1477.

Print shops were active not only on the Upper Rhine but also in the commercial centre of Cologne. Indeed, a direct line of descent links the pioneer of printing in Cologne, Ulrich Zell of Hanau (*c.* 1435–1503), to the cradle of the printed book, since Zell learned his trade as an apprentice to Fust and Schöffer in Mainz before settling in Cologne in 1464. He is thought to have been responsible for the printing there of Cicero's *De officiis* ('On Duties') the following year; this was the beginning of an extensive publishing programme that focused on theological and humanist texts, 95 per cent of them in Latin. In terms of the number of printed works produced, Cologne soon topped the list of German print shop sites. Trading cities offered particularly good opportunities for development for the art of printing. While Bamberg and Mainz produced only small numbers of printed books over the ensuing decades, major centres of trade such as Augsburg, Nuremberg and Lübeck witnessed a boom in the numbers of print shops.

However, the decisive factor in the spread of book printing was the route over the Alps and the outstanding and artistically independent book printing sector in Italy, which soon enriched the whole of Europe with its products. As early as 1465 the German printers Konrad Sweynheim (d. 1477) and Arnold Pannartz (d. 1477) were plying their trade in the Benedictine monastery of St Scholastica at Subiaco near Rome. Their first dated work (29 October 1465) was an

Cicero's *Liber de senectute* ('Book on Old Age'), which was appended to the same author's work *De Officiis* ('On Duties'), printed in Rome in 1469 by Konrad Sweynheim and Arnold Pannartz; the gold initial capital letter is embellished with multi-coloured tendrils that culminate in depictions of golden pollen

edition of the writings of the Church Father Lactantius (*c.* 260–*c.* 325). That same year saw the appearance of an edition of Cicero's *De oratore*. This was followed in 1467 by St Augustine of Hippo's *De civitate* ('The City of God'). This work clearly proved to be a bestseller for them, with one of the earliest customs documents for printed works recording that, in January 1468, the monastery sent no fewer than 60 copies of this book to Rome. Over the following years consignments of books ranging in value from 1400 to 3,000 ducats annually were dispatched from Subiaco to Rome.[50]

We know about the close links between the Roman curia and German book printers and bishops from a letter written by the Bishop of Aleria, Giovanni Andrea dei Bussi, dedicating a copy of the *Epistolae* of St Jerome, which was printed by Sweynheim and Pannartz in 1468, to Pope Paul II. In this dedication Bussi, who would later be appointed as the Vatican's first librarian, praised the invention of the art of printing and named Nicholas of Cusa as one of its key patrons: 'Germany is indeed worthy of being honoured and lauded down the centuries as the

BEATISSIMO PATRI PAVLO SE
CVNDO PONTIFICI MAXIMO.
DONIS NICOLAVS GERMANVS

This dedicatory initial letter shows a Benedictine monk, Nikolaus Germanus, presenting Pope Paul II with a copy of Ptolemy's *Cosmographia*, Ulm, 1482

place where this beneficial art was invented. This is also the reason why that most praiseworthy and blessed soul Nicholas of Cusa, the cardinal of St Peter ad Vincula, expressed the ardent wish that this sacred art [*sancta ars*], which was just emerging in Germany at the time, might also take root in Rome.'[51] Here Nicholas of Cusa is expressly identified as the person who facilitated the interchange of book printing technology between Germany and Italy and who promoted this 'sacred art'. Given that throughout his life Nicholas championed the idea of a standardised liturgy based on corresponding texts and advocated improved knowledge on the part of both priests and lay people, the potential of book printing was, of course, extremely opportune for his pastoral objectives. Rome remained a major centre of printing in Italy throughout the incunabula period, with more than 40 print shops being recorded operating there up to the year 1500. Some 25 of these employed German printers.

More than a few sons of patricians from Nuremberg or Augsburg were already studying the humanities, medicine or law at universities in northern Italy. However, in the second half of the 15th century, we also find a large number of itinerant craftsmen, architects and master builders working south of the Alps. The rich exchange of educated book printers between Germany and Italy over these decades therefore forms part of a complete cultural picture of the era.

After Rome, Venice in particular should also be cited as an important site of early printing. In 1469 Johann von Speyer was granted a monopoly on printing books in the city for a period of five years. However, as he died the very next year, his brother Wendelin carried on the work. As in other Italian cities, the majority of texts printed were those of the classical Latin writers and legal works. Of special significance are Wendelin's first Bible in Italian (1471) and – as an important document of Italian humanism printed in the vernacular – Petrarch's *Il Canzoniere* (1470). A clear, firm Antiqua type characterises works produced in Venice during these early years.

Another printer to work in Venice was Nicolas Jenson from Sommevoir near Troyes, who was sent to Mainz in 1458 by the *monetarius* (mint master) of King Charles VII of France to learn all about the new technology of printing. In Venice, from 1470 onwards, Jenson published the writings of the classical Latin authors and works of the Church Fathers in a particularly well-balanced Antiqua typeface. He ran his print shop, which was situated in the Fondaco dei Tedeschi (the headquarters of Venice's German trading community on the Grand Canal), as a partnership with two German merchants. Erhard Ratdolt from Augsburg also printed in Venice. He had previously worked in Nuremberg with the astronomer and book printer Johannes Regiomontanus, whose *Calendrium* he published in 1476 in an elegant Venetian Antiqua type with decorative letters and stylised leaf ornaments in both Latin and Italian. Another outstanding example of his art is Euclid's *Elementa geometriae* (May 1482). Yet the most important printer was undoubtedly the Italian Aldus Manutius (1449–1515), who in 1490 set up a print shop in Venice with the intention of publishing the Latin and Greek classics. His remarkable publications include the *Hypnerotomachia Poliphili*

The beginning of the Book of Genesis from the first Bible to appear in Italian, printed by Wendelin von Speyer in Venice in 1471

('Poliphilo's Strife of Love in a Dream'), which he printed in Italian in 1499. This difficult text full of mythological puzzles and allusions clearly posed a considerable challenge to Manutius, and his response was to create one of the most beautiful printed books of the Renaissance using a delicate and balanced Antiqua type and matching the text setting with equally simple and elegant woodcut illustrations. Here the illustrations are no longer merely a decorative adjunct but instead are an integral element that enhances the presentation of a literary text.

In Italy the art of printing that had originated in Germany developed further and took on a life of its own in both typography and design. Towards the end of the 15th century book design in northern Europe clearly came under the influence of apprentices and master printers returning from Italy. Foremost among them was Erhard Ratdolt, who after working for ten years in Venice, settled in Augsburg in 1486, bringing with him numerous Antiqua and Greek typefaces.

The significance of the art of book printing for the dissemination of knowledge was recognised above all by the universities. Consequently, the first printing press in France was located at the Sorbonne in 1470. The rector of the university, Johann Heynlein (also called Jean de Lapide, 1435–1496), and a fellow professor, Guillaume Fichet (1433–1480), tasked three German printing apprentices – Ulrich Gehring from Konstanz, Michael Friburger from Colmar and Martin Crantz from Strasbourg – with printing a series of classical and humanist texts, for which they used a relatively large Antiqua type. A number of other significant French printing centres followed the lead taken by Paris: Lyons (1473), Albi (1475) and Toulouse (1476). Less than a decade after Gutenberg's death his technology had spread to most European countries (see the map on page 164).

Finito che la nympha cum comitate blandiſſima hebbe il ſuo ben[i]
gno ſuaſo & multo acceptiſſima recordatióe, che la mia acrocoma Polia
propera & máſuetiſſima leuatoſe cum gli ſui feſteuóli, & facetiſſimi ſimu
lachri , ouero ſembianti, & cum punicante gene, & rubéte buccule da ho
neſto & uenerâte rubore ſuffuſe aptauaſe di uólere per omni uia ſatiſſare
di natura prompta ad omni uirtute, & dare opera alla honeſta petitione'.
Non che prima peroe ſe poteſſe cælare & dicio retinere alquáto che ella
intrinſicamente non ſuſpirulaſſe. Il quale dulciſſimo ſuſpirulo penetroe
reflectendo nel intimo del mio, immo ſuo core, per la uniforme conue-
nientia.   Quàle aduene a dui parimente participati & concordi litui. Et
ciaſcuna cum diuo obtuto reſpecta intrepidulamente, cum quegli ludi-
bondi & micanti ochii, Da fare (Ome) gli adamanti freſi in mille fragmé
ticuli. Cum pie & ſummiſſe uoce, & cum elegantiſſimi geſti decentemen
te reuerita ogni una, ritornoe al ſuo ſolatioſo ſedere ſupra il ſerpilaceo ſo
lo. La initiata opera ſequendo ſellularia . Cum accommodata pronunti
atio-

One of the most beautiful printed works of the Renaissance, the
Hypnerotomachia Poliphili ('Poliphilo's Strife of Love in a Dream'),
produced by Aldus Manutius in Venice in 1499

The book in Britain

The introduction of printing to England followed an independent course, in that it took place relatively late on and was concerned almost exclusively with English literature in the vernacular produced solely for an internal book market.[52] This situation also reflected the insular nature of England's cultural outlook in the 15th century, which was not as receptive towards the new ideas of Renaissance humanism as were more southern lands. Likewise the Pope was far enough away in Rome for independent and national religious usages to be cultivated. So it is not possible to trace the spread of printing to England back to Church or university roots, but rather to the activities of an erudite merchant, who in the second half of his life brought his rich business experiences as a wool trader – and at the same time his predilections as a translator and promoter of literature in English – to bear on this novel enterprise.

The history of the book, and equally the history of literature and education, in England is crucially determined by William Caxton (c. 1422–1491). This learned cloth merchant moved to the Netherlands while young and rose to eminence as a businessman in Bruges; from time to time he undertook diplomatic assignments for the Crown, becoming Head of the Guild of the Merchant Adventures and Governor of the English Nation at Bruges. He was active in the Netherlands, based in Flanders, Bruges and Ghent, for more than 30 years. His mercantile prominence made him a kind of Minister of Foreign Affairs for Britain and brought him into personal contact with the King and also with the King's sister, Margaret of York, Duchess of Burgundy, and other members of the royal entourage.

Margaret of York was herself greatly interested in literature and manuscripts, and Caxton repeatedly procured manuscripts for her and translated Raoul Lefèvre's *Receuils des histoires de Troye* into English at her behest. He completed the work of translation on 19 September 1471 during a stay in Cologne, as he writes himself in the prologue to the printed version (Bruges 1474): 'And ended and fynisshid in the holy cyte of Colen the XIX day of septembre the yere of our sayd lord god a thousand four honderd sixty and enleuen.' This statement establishes Caxton's residence in Cologne in 1471, and further documents found in the archives of that city confirm his presence in the following year.

His successor as printer at Westminster, Wynkyn de Worde, later asserted that Caxton had first printed the encyclopaedia *De proprietatibus rerum* (1472) by the Franciscan friar Bartholomaeus Anglicus in Cologne at this time; but it is probable that Caxton merely sponsored the publication of this encyclopaedia by his fellow countryman, also known as Bartholomew de Glanville. But it was apparently then that he learned to print in the workshop of the type-founder and master printer Johann Veldener.

Together with Veldener, he left Cologne at the end of 1472 and they moved to Bruges, where Veldener let Caxton print vernacular titles for the English market, amongst them his own translation of *The Recuyell of the Historyes of Troye* (c. 1473, H 7048). This is considered to be the first printed book in the English language, and its idiosyncratic Bastarda typeface from Veldener's workshop was to become typical for his subsequent publications.

After he had printed a further four titles, he returned to England in 1475/6 and set up his own workshop in the precincts of Westminster Abbey. There he began straightaway to print Chaucer's *Canterbury Tales*, dividing the work between two presses. In between he produced indulgences, just as Gutenberg had done, as a profitable sideline bringing rapid returns. He further attuned his publishing programme towards the English-speaking market, leaving liturgical and theological tomes in Latin and the works of classical authors to the continental incunabula printers. Amongst some 100 volumes, he offered *The Chronicles of England*, *The Mirrour of the World* (the first English book with woodcuts), *The Golden Legend* and *The Dictes and Sayengs of the Philosophers* (c. 1477). This last leans heavily on a manuscript by Guillaume de Tignoville entitled *Les ditz moraulz de philosophres* which had been translated into English by Anthony Woodville, second Earl Rivers. Caxton writes in an epilogue that for some incomprehensible reason Rivers had omitted to translate Socrates's statements about women, so that he had translated these himself and reinstated them. Twenty of his publications were translated into English by Caxton himself. Amongst these were assorted commissions from the English king, including the *Fayttes of Armes and of Chyualrye* (Westminster, 14 July 1489, GW 6648) translated from Christine de Pisan's *Faits d'armes et des chevalerie*. The French writer Christine de Pisan (1365–1430) was born at Venice and became celebrated for her allegorical fiction. Her political and historical record of Charles V and his court (1405) was also translated by Caxton. Henry VII placed his own manuscript of this work, still to be found in the British Library, at Caxton's disposal for the purposes of his translation. Such close connections with the royal house doubtless made the successful marketing of these titles easier to accomplish.

With the *Statutes* of Henry VII of 1490, Caxton published the first work of jurisprudence in English. His numerous prologues and post-scripts to his books reveal his close contacts with the highest circles in Westminster and London and his privileged access to the monarchy. That so many of his works evidently went through second and later editions suggests that in all probability he achieved considerable financial success as well. After his death in 1491, the workshop 'at the sign of the Red Pale' near Westminster Abbey continued to flourish under his colleague Wynkyn de Worde.

With the exception of Caxton the other early printers in England were foreigners who were nevertheless expressly encouraged in their activities through an act of parliament of Richard III in 1484. Not until the very different political climate of 1534 were foreign printers and booksellers prohibited from pursuing their occupations in England. Apart from Caxton, his colleague and successor the

Dutchman Wynkyn de Worde, who relocated the press to London's Fleet Street in 1500, is worthy of mention, as is Richard Pynson (d. 1530). From 1490 onwards Pynson, who came from Normandy, printed in a most agreeable typeface and from skilful woodcuts. Among his successes was the translation of Giovanni Boccaccio's *De casibus virorum illustrium* by John Lydgate (*c.* 1370–1450) entitled *The Fall of Princes* (London 1494, GW 4431).

Smaller printing offices were set up after about 1477 in nearby St Albans and at Oxford, where Theodoric Rood came from Cologne and printed some 20 classical and patristic texts with no great success; or as early as 1480 in the City of London itself, where John Lettou, a Lithuanian who had studied printing at Rome in about 1478/9, and William de Machlinia (i.e. Malines), practised together until 1482.

Caxton occupies a significant place in the history of printing and literature, but even this is outweighed by his contribution to the emergence of a standard English which overrides the various dialects. So Caxton serves as a significant promoter of a universal English literary language, to be compared in terms of the history of language to Martin Luther and the tremendous impact on the German language of his Bible translation. Lutheran writings were at first banned in England, and in the 1520s they were publicly burned. The first translations of the Bible into English by William Tyndale (1490–1536) had to be printed in Antwerp, Cologne, Mainz and Worms and then smuggled into England. The theologian Tyndale visited Luther in Wittenberg in 1524 and resided in the Netherlands after 1529. Closely following Luther's procedure for his German vernacular Bible, he translated first the New Testament and then the Old Testament in parts between 1525 and 1534. Arrested and executed under the Inquisition, he was unable to finish the work of translation. His *New Testament*, translated into English with marginal notes by Tyndale assisted by William Roye, was published in Cologne in 1525, with a second edition appearing from Worms in the following year.

The Pentateuch was published in Antwerp in 1530 as *The firste Boke of Moses called Genesis Newly correctyd and amendyd by W.T.*, and a new edition of the New Testament: *The newe Testament, dylygently corrected and compared with the Greke by Willyam Tyndale* appeared there in 1534. Tyndale's translation had a significance for the English language and the course of theology in England which corresponded to the impact of Luther's translation on the German language and continental theology.

After England, printing reached Stockholm in 1483, Istanbul in 1503, Salonika in 1515 and Moscow in 1553. Printing can be shown to have taken place in Goa (India) by 1556 and in Kazusa (Japan) by 1590. Although texts had been multiplied by taking rubbings since the 8th century in the Far East, it was not for a further eight centuries that Gutenberg's method of printing by means of a press became known to the advanced cultures in these parts of the world.

Two intellectual tendencies were of key importance in the spread of printing: the Renaissance and humanism that blossomed in the 15th century in Italy and the Reformation instigated by Martin Luther in the 16th century. The rapid spread of these ideas and the dissemination of the new communication technology can only be properly comprehended by appreciating how they underpinned and facilitated one another.

Humanism and printing
In an ode composed at the end of the 15th century, the German humanist Conrad Celtis (1459–1508) wrote that it was thanks to a son of the city of Mainz that the Germans no longer had to suffer taunts from the Italians about their alleged apathy towards intellectual enquiry. The art of printing, Celtis explained, had enabled them to connect with the intellectual greatness of the ancient world. And in much the same way as the Roman poet Virgil in his *Georgics*

had posited Italy's adoption of the Greek Muses and the art forms they embodied, Celtis now expressed the wish that the Muses, and with them the aptitude for true poetry and learning, might cross the Alps into the German-speaking lands. As early as 1486, the year in which Archduke Maximilian I of Austria was crowned King of the Romans, Celtis in another of his odes had implored the god Apollo, the patron deity of poets, to take up his lyre and move from Italy to Germany: 'O come, we beseech you, to our shores, just as you once visited the land of Italy; and may you then put all Barbarian language to flight and dissipate all darkness.'

Conrad Celtis was at pains to stress the difference between the uncultivated Barbarians with their clumsy language and the educated, civilised Romans. He saw this linguistic shortcoming as being tantamount to a cultural deficit. In doing so he was echoing the Italian humanists Francesco Petrarca (Petrarch, 1304–1374) and Lorenzo Valla (1406–1457), who stressed the civilising function of Latin. They prized Latin as the language of global culture and of learning and the liberal arts in general. In their view, however, language was not just the medium but at the same time both the origin (they used the term *semen*, 'seed') and itself the subject of educated discourse. The Latin language therefore became the hallmark of all true erudition (*eruditus*) and civilised behaviour (*civilitas*) and hence of all humane coexistence. They took the close connection between Latin and legal and ecclesiastical language as proof positive that they were correct in seeing Latin's fundamental character as being that of a vehicle of a particular cultural and intellectual mindset. Anyone who learned this language therefore became party to its inherent wisdom. By contrast, in the decline of Latin usage they saw a general intellectual decadence, pointing in this regard to Asia and North Africa after the fall of the Roman Empire. Just as the promotion of Latin became a national mission for the Italian humanists to re-establish a connection with the former greatness of Rome, so Celtis hoped that he might succeed in imparting the wisdom that was

Humanism

Humanism, which is associated with the European Renaissance, was characterised by an intensified interest in classical and Christian antiquity. An educational movement that aimed to revive the ideals of that earlier age, humanism began to exercise a formative influence on religious, political and social life, first in Italy from the 14th century and then in Central Europe. As a philosophical position, it soon came to embrace all aspects of existence. Antiquity was taken as the yardstick of all human endeavour, and even its aesthetic and stylistic criteria were adopted. In his book *Humanism*, Dieter Wuttke summarises the movement thus: 'In harking back to ancient, primarily classical, knowledge, which had at its core a consciousness of the dignity and obligations of the human being as a creature made in God's image, the principal concern of the humanists was to fashion a new knowledge, new consciousness and new wisdom that would make humanity ethically more mature and bring it closer to God.' (page 25 f.)

inherent in Latin to the German Empire and giving intellectuals there the opportunity to strive confidently to attain an equal footing with the educated peoples of the world. In the aforementioned ode, Celtis described how it might be possible for Germany to overcome its intellectual tardiness: the only way to do this, he claimed, was through Gutenberg's technological invention, which enabled 'characters to be cast from metal and taught people the art of how to write using reversed letters' – a description of the new technology that was as pithy as it was apt.[53] Anthologies and editions of ancient texts that were philologically accurate, appropriately structured and affordable would help to achieve this objective.

Erasmus of Rotterdam (*c.* 1466–1536) was just as appreciative as Celtis in his assessment of the prospects of book printing in educating the broad populace. In a letter in 1523 to the Alsatian theologian Johannes Botzheim (*c.* 1480–1524), he bemoaned the late intellectual flowering north of the Alps: 'When I was a boy the humanities had begun to put forth fresh shoots among the Italians; but because the printer's art was either not yet invented or was still known only to very few, nothing in the way of book came through

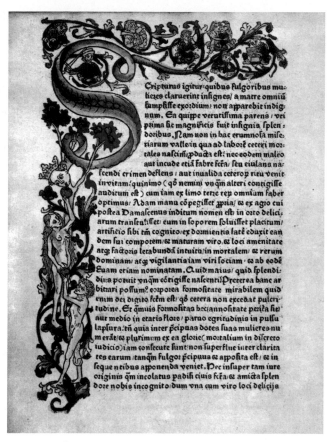

Opening page of Boccaccio's *De Claris Mulieribus* ('On Famous Women'), printed by Johann Zainer in Ulm in 1473, showing Eve's fall from grace and the serpent in the Garden of Eden as the capital letter 'S'

to us, and uninterrupted slumber graced the universal reign of those who taught ignorance instead of knowledge.'

After the art of printing became known, according to Erasmus the Italians employed the new technology more consistently and sensibly. Accordingly, in his *Adagia* he called for the technology to be given public support on his side of the Alps, too: 'If our northern princes were to patronise good learning as openly and honestly as their Italian counterparts, the serpents of Froben would be enjoying the same success as Aldus's dolphin in the bookshops. Under the motto "more haste, less speed" [*festina lente*], Aldus has managed to acquire both wealth and fame, and both of these are, I must say, richly deserved. Froben, on the other hand, who holds his staff upright and focuses upon nothing but public service, because he refuses to renounce the pure simplicity of the dove and evinces the cunning of the snake more in his printer's mark than in his way of conducting business, has become far more renowned than rich.'[54]

Erasmus is alluding here to the printer's marks of the famous book printers Aldus Manutius of Venice (a dolphin and anchor) and Johann Froben of Basle in Switzerland (two snakes coiling around a *caduceus*, a staff carried by heralds). Both men had played a significant role not only in disseminating Erasmus's writings but also in spreading the texts of antiquity in the spirit of the Renaissance and humanism.

The most frequently printed ancient texts during the incunabula period were the works of Cicero. Half of the 316 editions in existence were produced in Italy in the major printing cities of Rome, Venice and Milan but also Parma. Among these publications there is a preponderance of editions of Cicero's letters and his rhetorical works, which were hailed as representing a new artistic and stylistic ideal. Where Roman poets are concerned, we find 80 editions of Ovid, more than half of which are editions of the *Epistolae Heroidum*, which were used for teaching in schools.

In addition, the comedies of the playwright Terence were wide-spread; from 1470 Johannes Mentelin made these available in the German Empire, too. Johannes Grüninger (1455–1533) published a Latin edition of Terence in Strasbourg in 1496, followed by an extensively illustrated German edition in 1499. This was preceded by a Latin edition of Terence's works printed in Lyons in 1493 by Johann Trechsel (d. 1498) which, with its 159 illustrations, is regarded as one of the major achievements of early French typography. Trechsel's edition is of huge importance not only for textual criticism and the history of book production but also for theatre studies and the history of costume design. The title woodcut is the first ever portrayal of a Terence-Stage (a continuous façade divided into a series of curtained openings, each representing the house of a different character) and of a Gothic comedy playhouse, and the full-page scene-setting images at the start of each comedy were the first depictions in book illustration of characters in a drama. The text and the accompanying commentary are set in two columns and vividly illustrated with 158 woodcuts within the text.

In 1498 Johannes Grüninger's print shop also produced a lavishly illustrated edition of the works of Horace edited by Jakob Locher. Petrarch counted the writer of the *Odes* among his favourite authors, while in 1482 Landino had published the first humanist commentary on Horace, which was soon followed by several others. Among the German humanists, Conrad Celtis was the first to discover Horace when he included an introduction to Horace's prosody in his 1486 study *Ars versificandi* ('The Art of Versification').

The writings of Virgil occupy a quantitatively exceptional position; even in classical antiquity – at the special behest of the Roman Emperor Augustus – they enjoyed widespread distribution, initially on scrolls of papyrus, while in the 4th century AD these were transferred on to parchment codices. A total of eight such codices, more than for any other ancient author, have survived from late antiquity. After some 50 generations had repeatedly transcribed these texts, in 1469 the first printed edition was published in Rome, and thereafter scarcely a year went by in which at least one edition of Virgil did not appear. Between 1469 and the end of the incunabula period there were no fewer than 81 printings of the poet's complete works (*Opera omnia*) alone. Giovanni Andrea dei Bussi obtained the *editio princeps* (the first printed edition) from the printers Konrad Sweynheim and Arnold Pannartz in Rome; this included all the pieces of scholarly apparatus that were commonly found in manuscript transcriptions of Virgil's works in the Middle Ages – Aelius Donatus's *Life of Virgil*, the verses of the *Appendix Vergiliana* plus other minor works (*opuscula*) that were attributed to him. From 1475 the textual commentary by Servius was also usually included. As in other matters, the printers followed the manuscripts when it came to the arrangement of the commentary within the typeset text: the main text was framed by the commentary, which was set in a smaller point size. The current practice of setting the commentary beneath the text only became established in the 17th century.

However, it was not only works of ancient literature that were published but also those of jurisprudence and the natural sciences. As early as 24 May 1475 Peter Schöffer completed printing the *Institutiones Justiniani*, the setting of which once again followed manuscript practice, with the text in a larger point size surrounded by the commentary in a smaller size. The *Gesamtkatalog der Wiegendrucke* ('Complete Catalogue of Incunabula') or *GW*, compiled in 1925, lists some 200 editions of Justinian's *Corpus Iuris Civilis*, most of which appeared in Venice, although editions of Roman law were also printed in Strasbourg by Heinrich Eggestein (*c.* 1420–1488) and in Nuremberg by Anton Koberger (d. 1513).

The *Historia naturalis* ('Natural History') of Pliny the Elder (AD 23–79), a compendium of ancient physics, mathematics, medicine, zoology, geography and astronomy, was first published in a printed version in Venice in 1469 by Johann von Speyer and went through 15 reprintings up to 1500. This encyclopaedic overview of natural

Codex Justinianus, printed in Mainz by Peter Schöffer, 1475

Poggy Florentini Oratoris eloquentissimi · ac secretary
apłici · facetiaꝛ liber incipit feliciter · ⸿ Prefatio

Vltos futuros esse arbitror qui has nŕas
confabulationes cum ut res leues & uiro
graui indignas deprehendãt · tum ut in
eis ornatiore dicendi modum & maiore
eloquentiam requirant · quibꝫ ego si re-
spondeã legisse me nostros maiores pru-
dentissimos ac doctissimos uiros facetýs iocis & fabulis
delectatos non repꝫhensionem sed laudem meruisse · satis
mihi factum ad illoꝛ existimatione putabo · Nã qui mihi
turpe esse putem ac in re quandoquide in ceteris nequeo
illoꝛ imitatione sequi · & hoc idem tempus quod reliqui
in circulis & cetu hominũ confabulando conterũt in scribendi cura consumere · pꝫsertim cum neꝫ inhonestus labor
sit & legentes aliqua iocunditate possit afficere · Honestũ
est eñ ac ferme necessariũ certeꝫ semp sapiétes laudarũt
mente nostrã varýs cogitationibꝫ ac molestýs oppressam
recreari quandoꝗ a cõtinuis curis · & eã iocandi genere
ad hilaritatem remissionemꝗ conuerti · Eloquétiam vero
in rebꝫ infimis vel in ýs in quibꝫ ad uerbum vel facetie ex-
primende sunt vel alioꝛ dicta referanda querere homìnis
nimiũ curiosi ee uidet · Sũt eñ quedã ꝗ oznatius nequnt
describi cũ ita recensenda sint quéadmodũ ea protulerũt
hý qui in cõfabulationibꝫ conitjunt · Existimabũt aliqui
forsan hanc meã excusatione ab ingený culpa esse pꝫfectã
quibꝫ ego quoꝗ assentior modo ipfi eadem oznatius poli-
tiusꝗ describant · quod ut faciat exhortor quo lingua latina etiã leuiori in rebꝫ hac nostra etate fiat opulentior ·
⸿Proderit eñ & ad eloquentiam & doctrinã ea scribendi
exercitacõ · Ego quidé expiri volui an multa ꝗ latine dici
difficulter existimant non absurde scribi posse uiderent

Poggio Bracciolini: *Facetiae*, printed by Anton Koberger in Nuremberg, c.
1472, fol. 2 recto: preface, with a blue Initial 'M' on a gold background

history was in evidence throughout the Middle Ages, and over 200 manuscripts have survived to the present day. The medical works of the Greek physician Galen (AD 129–c. 199) also attracted considerable interest, particularly in Italy: some of his writings in Latin translation appeared in the collection *Articella*, with a larger selection published in 1490 in Venice, followed by a Greek edition of the *Therapeutica* in 1500. In the 16th century these publications formed the basis of a philological-literary or humanist medicine, which operated according to the dictum of *ad fontes* ('back to the sources') and which endeavoured to render the medical knowledge of antiquity, namely that of ancient Greece, relevant and useful to the contemporary world.

Book printing and the Reformation

'Doctor Martinus Luther announced: "Printing is *summum et postremum donum* [the greatest and ultimate gift] through which God wants the whole world, to the ends of the earth, to know the roots of true religion and to broadcast it in every language. Printing is the last flicker of the flame that glows before the extinction of this world."' With this enthusiastic appraisal, Johannes Aurifaber brought to a close his 1566 edition of Martin Luther's *Tischreden* ('Table Talks') in which he conveyed Luther's reforming ideas through clear examples presented in a popular way. In citing this dictum of Luther's, Aurifaber (1519–1575, also known by the Germanised form of his name, Johann Goldschmid) was attesting to the important role that printing played in spreading not only the ideas of the Reformation but, above all, the Gospels.

Indeed, the history of the printing press is inextricably bound up with the spread of the Holy Scriptures. As we have already seen, in the early 1450s Johannes Gutenberg printed the Vulgate, the transcription into Latin of the Bible by St Jerome that had been the standard version since late antiquity; this was an opulent edition set in the imposing Textura font. In the 15th century, a total of 94 complete

German Bible editions before Luther

Strasbourg	1466	Johannes Mentelin
Strasbourg	1470	Heinrich Eggestein
Augsburg	1475	Günther Zainer
Augsburg	1475	Jodokus Pflanzmann
Nuremberg	1476/78	Johann Sensenschmidt
Augsburg	1477	Günther Zainer
Augsburg	1477	Anton Sorg
Cologne (Lower Saxon)	1478	Bartholomaeus von Unkel
Cologne (Lower Rhenish)	1478	Bartholomaeus von Unkel
Augsburg	1480	Anton Sorg
Nuremberg	1483	Anton Koberger
Strasbourg	1485	Johannes Grüninger
Augsburg	1487	Johann Schönsperger
Augsburg	1490	Johann Schönsperger
Lübeck (Low German)	1494	The Lübeck Bible
Augsburg	1507	Johann and Silvan Otmar
Augsburg	1518	Johann and Silvan Otmar
Halberstadt (Low German)	1522	The Halberstadt Bible

editions of the Vulgate Bible were printed, of which 22 were directly in the style of the Gutenberg Bible.

The earliest undated printed Bible from Strasbourg was also a 49-line Vulgate. The copy in the university library in Freiburg was rubricated in 1460 and 1461, the work being produced by the pioneer of printing in Strasbourg, Johannes Mentelin. Mentelin came from Sélestadt in northern Alsace, where he is recorded as being a calligrapher and book scribe by trade (*Goldschreiber*) as well as a notary. In around 1447 he was granted right of citizenship in Strasbourg and most likely began printing there from 1458 onwards. In 1466 he produced the first complete German-language Bible, based on a translation (now lost) that was already over a hundred years old. But because Mentelin's Bible followed the Latin model closely, the

German text could actually only be understood by those who had a good command of Latin grammar. In addition, certain words and forms of words were already archaic.

Yet, despite its outmoded language, this Bible was reprinted 13 times up to 1518, nine of these reprints originating from Augsburg alone. In the second and third editions – printed respectively in 1470 by Heinrich Eggestein in Strasbourg and in 1475 by Jodokus Pflanzmann – individual words that were no longer in common usage were replaced, although only the fourth edition, which appeared in 1475 printed by Günther Zainer in Augsburg, was subjected to a thorough text revision on the basis of the Vulgate. In a publisher's advertisement of 1476 (one of the first book dealer advertisements ever printed), Zainer sets out his wares as follows: 'The book of the German Bible, with illustrations, corrected and made right with great diligence. In as much as all unfamiliar German words that are not intelligible, which appeared in the first small Bibles to be printed, have now been completely expunged and revised according to the Latin original.'

In addition to improving and modernising the text itself, Zainer also added illustrations to a German Bible for the first time, in the form of 73 pictorial initials, one at the beginning of each book of the Bible. They depict 45 biblical scenes, portraits of the authors of certain books and the handing down of the apostolic letters. Zainer's refined Gotico-Antiqua type creates an overall picture of composure and balance, an impression that is compounded by the liberal spacing of the two columns of text with a broad gutter in between.

The transition from this kind of illustrative book decoration to narrative woodcuts that not only edified Christians looking at them but also stimulated them to read the Bible, and which were designed to facilitate understanding, is effected by two Bibles printed respectively in the Lower Saxon and Lower Rhenish dialects, which appeared in 1478 in Cologne and were most probably the work of Bartholomaeus von Unkel, at the behest of a publishing consortium founded by the noblemen Johann Helmann and Arnold

Hartmann Schedel's *Weltchronik*

One of the most important incunabula is the *Weltchronik* ('Chronicle of the World') by Hartmann Schedel (1440–1514), the city physician of Nuremberg. Around 1,400 copies of the Latin version of his text plus 700 of the German edition were printed in the city in 1493 by the prominent publisher Anton Koberger. The 'Chronicle' is known for its many, often hitherto unseen, city views reproduced in woodcuts. However, only a small proportion of them are authentic; for example, a single woodcut did service for the cityscapes of such diverse places as Mainz, Naples, Aquila, Bologna and Lyons. Other illustrations, such as those for Regensburg or Nuremberg, are still greatly admired even today for their detailed accuracy. The woodcuts were created in the workshop of Michael Wohlgemut and his stepson Wilhelm Pleydenwurff, and because Albrecht Dürer was apprenticed to them in the period 1486–1489 speculation has always been rife that the young Dürer was also involved in making the preliminary drawings for the illustrations that appeared in the 'Chronicle'.

Hartmann Schedel divided his chronicle into seven sections, in accordance with the story of the Creation. The first aeon presented the Creation Myth itself, while the second began with the building of Noah's Ark and ended with the departure of Lot from the city of Sodom as it was consumed by fire and brimstone. The third aeon contains the story of Abraham, Moses, Joseph and King Saul. This section includes the city views of Paris, Mainz, Venice and Padua, since Schedel traced the founding of these places back to the Trojans.

The fourth aeon began with King David and King Solomon and ended with the destruction of Jerusalem. This is combined with the history of Rome and disquisitions on various ancient poets and philosophers. The fifth aeon spans the period from the Babylonian captivity of the Jews to the beheading of John the Baptist. The sixth aeon begins with the birth of Christ and ends in the present day, thus spanning 1,500 years of history; accordingly, this is the most extensive section, at over 300 pages. This is the chapter where we find most of the authentic city views, presented in the order of their founding: Regensburg, Vienna, Nuremberg, Metz, Geneva, Constantinople, Budapest, Strasbourg and so on. The seventh aeon includes salvatory observations on the end of the world, thereby neatly tying in with the opening section on the Creation.

Hartmann Schedel's *Weltchronik*, Nuremberg 1493: the birth of Eve

Salmonster from Cologne. They were printed by Anton Koberger from Nuremberg. The Lower Saxon edition has 113 illustrations, whereas the Lower Rhenish has 123. The woodcuts were particularly influenced by the 'author images' (showing the evangelists, prophets and apostles) in Zainer's edition but also took their cue from miniatures from Bible manuscripts and historical Bibles from the region around Cologne and the Low Countries.

The clearly narrative nature of the illustrations and an extensive foreword, which exhorts every Christian to read the Bible, demonstrate the new aim of the *devotio moderna*, namely to bring the Word of God within reach of lay people as well. In all probability the publishers were the Brethren of the Common Life and the Cologne Carthusians, who in the foreword also invoked the traditional pictorial biblical images in monasteries and churches, which were now likewise to serve the purpose of educating believers. The rendering of Latin into the two dialects that were commonly spoken within the Diocese of Cologne also testifies to the topicality of this initiative. The dominant, two-column woodcuts characterise these Bibles, which are also embellished with further elaborate borders.

The illustration on page 119 shows the beginning of the Book of Genesis, with the story of the Creation and the forming of Eve out of one of Adam's ribs. This pictorial motif, which was taken from illuminations in manuscripts, was an extremely popular subject for woodcuts and was widespread not only in numerous other Bibles but also in encyclopaedias such as the Hartmann Schedel's *Weltchronik* of 1493.

The partner in producing the Cologne Bibles, the leading Nuremberg publisher Anton Koberger, had acquired the woodblock illustrations in Cologne and reprinted 109 of them in his Bible of 1483, having them coloured in his own print shop. The text is based on Zainer's edition but was itself in turn improved through reference to the Latin Vulgate. In his colophon, on the verso of sheet 586, Koberger is at pains to point this feature out: 'Made good in accordance with to the Latin text [...] and furnished with beautiful illustrations.' Koberger entertained far-reaching business connections in Europe and evidently produced a large print run. The type he employed was a pronounced Bastarda font that still displayed some affinities with Upper Rhenish cursive handwriting but which also represented a clear precursor form of a black-letter font that originated in Nuremberg. As such, the typography of Koberger's Bible is strikingly different in appearance from the contemporaneous

Latin-language texts set in Antiqua (cf. the example featuring Noah's Ark shown on page 122).

Like the manuscript Bibles, these printed works were beautifully appointed and sold for considerable sums, which surely put them beyond the financial means of the common man. Simpler 'utilitarian Bibles' were printed in Augsburg in 1507 and 1518 by Johann and Silvan Otmar, who reused the woodcuts from an edition printed by Johann Schönsperger in 1487.

The existence of 18 different German-language editions of the Bible before Luther is quite remarkable; even so, the fact that they only had a limited impact was undoubtedly down to their high cost, the archaic nature of the language used and on the prevailing translation principle of *verbum e verbo* ('word for word'), which adhered slavishly to the Latin original and as a result gave rise to numerous difficulties of comprehension and distortions of meaning. Consequently, the German text was only intelligible to someone who was capable in any case of reading the Latin text. Because the Church arrogated to itself sole authority to conduct textual exegesis of the Holy Scriptures, there was little incentive to acquire these editions.

It was only the new weight that Luther conferred on the Scriptures in both theological thought and ecclesiastical practice, the principles that the Scriptures alone had validity in questions of faith and that lay people were mature enough to read the Bible on their own and to distinguish between revealed truth and the bogus practices of the 'old Church', together with the sheer creative power of Luther's language in rendering the original Greek and Hebrew texts into German, that lent his translation of the Bible an unprecedented resonance. From 1522 until Luther's death in 1546 more than 300 editions of the Bible in High German appeared, with a total print run of over half a million copies – a figure hitherto unknown in what was still an embryonic book-purchasing market and a situation of far from universal literacy. Luther's writings represented a third

hundert vnd zwelff iar vnd ſtarb.Enos aber ſe
bet.lȥ.iar vñ gepar caynan.nach des gepurd
ſebet er achthundert vnd fünffȥehen iar vñ gepar ſün vnd töchter.vnd alle dye tag enos ſeyn
worden newnhundert vnd fünff iar vnd ſtarb.
Vnd caynan ſebet ſibentȥig iar vnd gepar ma
ſalehel.vnnd caynan ſebet ſarnach.So er gepar
malalehel achthundert vñ viertȥig iar vñ gepar
ſün vñ töchter.vnd alle die tag caynan wurden
newnhundert vnd ȥehen iar vñ ſtarb.Waiñ ma
ſaſchel ſebet fünff vñ ſechtȥig iar vnd gepar iared . vnnd maſaſchel ſebet ſarnach. So er gepar iared achthundert vñ dreyſſig iar.vñ gepar
ſün vñ töchter.vnd alle die tag maſaſchel wurden achthundert vñ fünff vñ newntȥig iar vnd
ſtarb. Vñ iared ſebet hundert vñ ȥwey vñ ſech
tȥig iar.vñ gepar enoch.vñ iared ſebet ſarnach
So er gepar Enoch achthundert iar vnd gepar
ſün vñ töchter vnd alle die tag iared ſeyn wor
den newnhundert vnd ȥwey vñ ſechtȥig iar vnd
ſtarb.aber enoch ſebet fünff vnnd ſechtȥig iar

vñ gepar mathuſolé .vñ enoch gieng mit got.vñ
enoch ſebet ſarnach So er gepar matuſalé drey
hundert iar vñ gepar ſün vnd töchter vñ alle ſy
tag enoch wurde gemacht dreyhndert vñ fünf
vñ ſechtȥig iar.vñ er gieng mit got vñ erſchyn
nit.wañ got der nä oder erhube in. Vñ matuſa-
ſem ſebet hundert vnd ſiben vñ achtȥig iar. vnd
gebar ſamech vñ mathuſalé ſozach.So er
gepar ſamech ſibenhundert vñ ȥwey vñ achtȥig
iar.vnd gepar ſün vnd töchter.vnd alle dye tag
matuſalé wurden newnhundert vnd newn vnd
ſechtȥig iar.vnd ſtarb. Wann ſamech ſebet hüdert vnd ȥwey vnd achtȥig iar.end gepar eynen
ſün.vñ hieſ ſei namé noe ſagend.Der wirt vnſ
tröſté vo de arbeite vñ vo de werckē vnſer hend
i der erde.Ser.Serherr hat geflücht.end ſamech
ſebr ſarnach .So er gebar noe fünff hüdert vñ
fünff vñ newntȥig iar vñ gepar ſün vñ töchter.vñ
alle ſy tag ſamech wurde ſibehüdert vñ ſibē vñ
ſibētȥig iar vñ ſtarb.Noe aber ſo er alt ward
fünf hüdert iar ſo gebar.er ſem cham vñ iaphet

ARCHA   NOE E

Das .VI. Capitel.wie
got der herr vmb boſheit willen der menſchen
die werlt hreſ vergeen in dem waſſer vnd hyeſ
noe ein archen machen ſich vnd die ſeynen dar-
ȥu zuenthalten.

ANS do dye menſchen
hette angefange manigualtig ȥewer
dē auf der erdē vñ hette geborn töch

er.die ſün gotz ſahe die töchter der menſchē
ſȥ ware ſchön ſy name in weyber auſ allē dē
die ſy erwelten.Vñ got der ſprach.Mein geiſt
wirt nit beſeybē in den menſchē ewigklich.waṅ
er iſt fleyſch.Vnnd ſeyn tag werden ȥwaintȥig
vñ hündert iar.Vñ i dē tage warē ryſen auf der
erdē.Vñ darnach do dye ſün gottes warē einge
gange ȥu dē töchtern der meſchē.vñ ſy gebarē
diſ ſeu dy gewaltige vo der welt der berümtē
maṅ.do aber got ſah dȥ vil ebeſs der menſchē

Noah's Ark, in a woodcut from the *Biblia Germanica* (Anton Koberger,
Nuremberg, 1483), the ninth Bible to be printed in German

of all German-language book production in the first half of the 16th century.

While Luther's internal exile at Wartburg and, according to Luther's own testimony, an urgent request to do so by the humanist Philipp Melanchthon were the immediate catalysts of his Bible translation, the root causes lay much deeper. Luther's candid and unequivocal commitment to Holy Scripture as the supreme authority in matters of faith and his stubborn recourse to the Bible to corroborate his arguments had stimulated a great need for a comprehensible translation into the vernacular. At the centre of his Bible translation stood his humanistic reversion to the sources, namely the original Greek and Hebrew texts, whereas previous translations had relied solely on the Latin Vulgate. He freed himself from slavish imitation of Latin diction by translating 'not word for word, but rather meaning for meaning', an approach that Heinrich Steinhöwel had already recommended for his prose translations in the late 15th century. In his tract *Ein Sendbrief vom Dolmetschen* ('Treatise on the Art of Translation', 1530), Luther attacked the 'literalists' (*Buchstabilisten*): 'For one ought not to interrogate the letters in the Latin language in order to find out how to say something in German the way these asses do; instead, one should ask mothers at home, children on the street, and the common man at the marketplace, and look at their mouths to see how they talk, and then translate accordingly. Then they will understand it and recognise that one is speaking German to them.'

By way of example, Luther did not translate the passage from the Gospel According to St Matthew (12.34) '*Ex abundantia cordis os loquitur*' literally as '*Aus dem Überfluß des hertzen redet der mund*' ('For out of the abundance of the heart, the mouth speaks') but instead rendered it more accessibly as '*Wes das hertz vol ist, des geht der mund über*' ('If your heart is brimming over with something, then it will flow out of your mouth'). Similarly, Mark 14:4 ('*Ut quid perditio ista ungenti facta est*') was now translated not as '*Warum ist dise verlierung der salben geschehen?*' ('Wherefore has this waste of the ointment occurred?') but as '*Es ist schade um die Salbe*' ('Shame about the waste of ointment').

In cases where the sense of the original could not be conveyed by a loose translation (because, as Luther put it, the phraseology of the original 'had more to it', that is, it harboured a more subtle, complex meaning), then he preferred a literal translation. For him, the paramount guiding principle was to put across the 'sense' of the text faithfully and to do so as painstakingly as he could, 'to the best of my abilities and as conscientiously as possible', as he expressed it in the *Sendbrief.* He worked from the premise that Scripture was its own best interpreter ('*scriptura sui ipsius interpres*') and hence that when problems arose in translating one needed to consult comparable passages. He looked at individual verses within the context of the entire Bible, and to interpret them he applied his method of circular hermeneutic analysis, proceeding from the specific to the whole, and from the letter to the spirit. The prime example of this intertwining of linguistic and theological argumentation is his translation of the following passage from St Paul's Epistle to the Romans 3:28: 'We therefore hold that a man is justified not by the works of the law, but through faith alone.' Luther spiritedly countered the objections that the word 'solely' was not to be found in either the Greek original or the Latin Vulgate by maintaining that the only way of clearly conveying a 'key tenet of Christian teaching' was through the introduction of 'solely' or 'alone'. Luther was referring here to the central message of Paul's epistles, that God could not be influenced in His dispensation of mercy by good works.

Pamphlets

It was not only Luther's Bible and his principal tracts promoting the Reformation that were published but also texts written by his fellow campaigners and supporters. Especially noteworthy in this context are the pamphlets, couched in the form of dialogues, issued by Ulrich von Hutten (1488–1523) or Hans Sachs (1494–1576).

Triumphus Veritatis, a pamphlet printed in 1524 probably in Zurich; here the victory of the Reformation is shown as the triumph of the 'true gospel'

The didactic character of this dialogue form, which had its origins in Latin literature, proved to be particularly beneficial in spreading the new reforming ideas. Fundamental questions of theology are discussed in a question-and-answer format that was easy for everyone to understand. In a work published by Hans Sachs in Nuremberg in 1524, for example, a canon and a cobbler engage in a debate; in this dialogue the canon betrays his true self out of his own mouth as being superficial and unthinking, whereas the cobbler, Hans, is shown to be a staunch Christian. This dialogue touches upon three problematic areas that Luther also broached in his 1520 treatise *An den christlichen Adel deutscher Nation* ('To the Christian Nobility of the German Nation'): the exclusive right of the Pope to interpret the Bible and to convene a council, and the supremacy of spiritual authority over the secular.

Representatives of both sides of the denominational divide appear in these prose dialogues and characterise themselves through their words and actions. In the process, not just purely theological questions take centre stage but also the effects of religious conduct on the business of everyday life – for example, in dialogues concerning the practices of usury and false fasting or the oppression and exploitation of the peasant classes. These pamphlets are therefore also fundamentally important in laying the intellectual groundwork for, and taking issue with, the German Peasants' War of 1524–5.

Both the propagandistic tracts of the Reformation and the polemical writings of the 'old' – that is, the Roman Catholic – Church are often quite extraordinarily drastic in their pictorial images. The graphically expressive woodcuts serve to emphasise the point once more that these texts were, in the great majority of cases, disseminated by being read out loud. One especially impressive pamphlet concerning the spread of the evangelical faith is a tract by Hans Heinrich Freiermut, almost certainly printed in Zurich in 1524, which depicts the *Triumphus Veritatis/Sick der warheyt* ('Triumph of the Truth'). The woodcut on the title page shows – like some portrayal of the Day of Judgement – the Pope and his confederate the Devil being cast out of heaven by the angels.

In a second woodcut (see page 125), printed from two woodblocks, the victory of the 'true gospel' is shown as a triumphal procession. A group of patriarchs, prophets and apostles are seen carrying the 'Sepulchre of Holy Scripture', concealed within a shrine, into a walled city to the sound of a trumpet fanfare and the 'cries of gratitude of the common people'. They are followed by the Protestant reformer Ulrich von Hutten, who is leading various clerics of the old Church, including the Pope and his bishops as well as a number of prominent Catholic theologians, in chains. They are portrayed satirically with animals' heads; for instance, the Franciscan Thomas Murner is seen in the guise of a cat, Hieronymus Emser as a goat and Johannes Eck as a pig (this is a visual pun on his title and name: 'Dr Eck' = *Dreck* [the German word for filth]). The Reformation leaders Luther and Karlstadt walk ahead of the triumphal chariot of Christ. Thus, the conquest of the old Church and the triumphal procession of the Word of God are celebrated in this succinct pictorial formulation.

In many cases the Reformation pamphlets also picked up on quite general themes that were live issues at the time – as, for instance, in

1523 the widespread fear of a Great Flood. As a result of a 'grand conjunction' of the planets Saturn and Jupiter under the zodiacal sign of Pisces, an ominous constellation of stars which recurred only every 960 years was predicted for 1524, triggering fear of a deluge throughout Europe. We know of hundreds of pamphlets from this time from Italy and the German-speaking lands that stirred up hysteria about this. In the pamphlet reproduced on page 128, these fears are linked with the upheaval afflicting the Church and the impending threat of a peasants' revolt. The figure of Saturn holding a flag and scythe is seen leading a mob of armed peasants, while following behind Jupiter, who is wearing a crown and wielding a sceptre, we see the Pope and the senior Catholic clergy. Fear that the empire and the Church might break apart, combined with a general belief in all manner of portents, fuelled public uncertainty.

Book printing also created completely new possibilities in the realm of cartography. After the 1490s had seen the appearance of the first maps of Germany and the wider world as broadsheets, the Holy Year of 1500 in particular prompted mass production by printers of maps showing the pilgrimage routes to Rome. The image on page 130 shows a 1533 reprint by Albrecht Glockendon of a map originally made by Erhard Etzlaub in 1501. Its title reads as follows: 'The highways through the [Holy] Roman Empire from one kingdom adjoining German lands to the next, marked out with dots.' Etzlaub showed the routes to Rome in the form of dotted lines, with each dot corresponding to a distance of a German mile, around 7.4 kilometres. The map is in a 'south-up' orientation, in other words with the destination of Rome being situated at the top edge. The city of Nuremberg lies roughly in the middle of the network of roads depicted. The legend below explains to the user that the orientation between each of the cities can be determined by placing a compass on the map. Even at the time, Etzlaub's work was much praised for giving a very precise rendition of the distances between cities and the courses of rivers. It is interesting to note that Martin Luther, on his

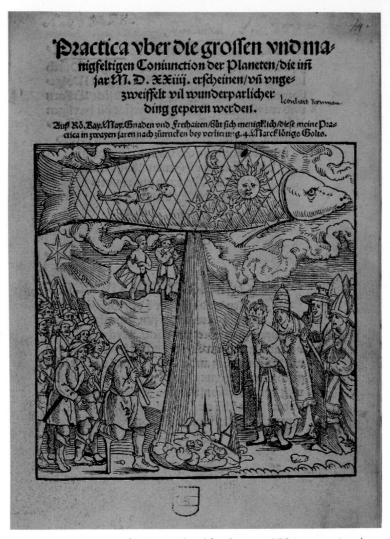

Astrological prophesy of a Great Flood for the year 1524, one example of the many warning pamphlets that were printed in 1523

famous journey to Rome, used one of the routes drawn on Etzlaub's maps.

The first three decades of the 16th century saw the publication of some 9,000 pamphlets. From 1517, the start of the Reformation, 17 per cent of all titles printed were pamphlets. Within a year of their promulgation, the '12 Articles' of the rebellious peasants had been published in over 24 editions that we know of, from 18 printers in 15 different cities. Between 1519 and 1522 the proportion of texts in the vernacular increased sevenfold, and this is undoubtedly associated with a greater interest in subject matters and a developing culture of reading. Even though the print runs of pamphlets only began at 500 copies, their impact was disproportionately greater, since in many places they were read out loud and discussed by local communities. So, for example, we know that Luther's reformist hymns were initially disseminated in all cities in an edition of just 400 and were made accessible to all those believers who were interested by being sung during parish church services. This practice is made vividly clear in a Reformation pamphlet of 1524, which begins with what might at first sight appear to be a paradoxical sentence: 'Dear reader, if you cannot read, then seek out a young man who can read this text out to you.' The driver behind the spread of the ideas of the Reformation was the printed word, the effect of which was then increased exponentially when the texts were made more widely known through sermons and hymns.

Newe Zeytungen

From the beginning of the 15th century the woodcut was used to rub, and later print, images and short texts on to sheets of paper. As we have seen, this technique was used to produce pilgrimage souvenirs and small pictures of saints as well as playing cards. Contemporaneous with the introduction of printing with movable type we also find typographical broadsheets. The advent of type printing saw the

A 1533 copy of Erhard Etzlaub's map of the pilgrimage routes leading to Rome, 1501; this 'south-up' map was initially used by pilgrims journeying to Rome in 1500 and was subsequently reprinted by Albrecht Glockendon in Nuremberg in large numbers for use by merchants and other travellers

calendar become a true mass-market article. As single-leaf prints they could be hung in people's living rooms and consulted on a daily basis. For this reason only a handful of examples have survived to the present day. Some calendars showed nothing but dates and symbols – perhaps denoting Sundays and working days, or auspicious dates on which to undergo bloodletting – which were intelligible even to those who were less adept at reading. Alongside these were practical pamphlets alerting people to counterfeit coins or reporting on acts of war. In the 1480s and 1490s the number of broadsheets containing sensational items of news such as miraculous births or reports about manifestations of imperial power increased markedly. From their headings they became known as '*Newe Zeytungen*', with the Middle High German word *Zeytung* initially denoting simply 'news' (it is cognate with the archaic English word 'tidings'), but over time the word became an eponym for the new medium itself: 'newspaper'. The first lines of the broadsheets often speak in sensational terms about 'shocking', 'glad' or 'new' tidings. In contrast to the regular press, which only came into being in the 17th century, these sheets are devoted solely to a single event and were aimed in each case at a specific audience. In addition to the news the *Zeytung* generally also included an informative woodcut. The text was often in the form of a rhyme, suggesting that they were intended for reading aloud in public. These prototype newspapers reported on natural disasters (see the Great Flood warning on page 128), changes in the law or the looming threat of war. In the run-up to the Thirty Years' War (1618–48), for instance, this popular medium played an important role. Certain rulers also used the broadsheets to spread political propaganda and influence public opinion.

Another medium – the most popular of the period with a sphere of influence even wider than that of the broadsheets – was that known as '*Feldmären*'. These were printed folk songs with topical themes. Some of these songs, mostly from unknown authors, reveal a direct dependence upon official pronouncements or are official edicts set in verse. However, Emperor Maximilian (1459–1519) did not merely use printed pamphlets to influence internal political opinion within the Holy Roman Empire but he was also behind a particular form of psychological warfare: in his stand-off with the Republic of Venice between 1509 and 1511 he deployed propaganda pamphlets printed in Italian in an attempt to stir up the ordinary people of Venice against their masters. In carefully crafted language he promised them 'freedom and equality' and encouraged the populace to rise up against the 'tyrants'. These pamphlets were presumably shot behind enemy lines wrapped around arrows, although (according to a contemporary account by Marino Sanuto) most reached their intended target by being distributed directly within Venice, left in the entrances to churches by Maximilian's agents in the city. One of these pamphlets, dated 1 August 1511 and probably printed in Augsburg, can still be seen in the Museo Correr in Venice (Sign.: DOC Cicogna 2281).

Over time, these *Newe Zeytungen* and pamphlets on single events evolved into periodical publications covering particular occurrences, prominent among which were, of course, the Reformation, the Counter-Reformation and the lead-up to the Thirty Years' War, a period of furious propagandising. In turn, these were to develop at the start of the 17th century into publications which appeared at regular intervals and which furnished a particular region or a particular readership with information, initially along the main postal routes that had been established by the princely house of Thurn und Taxis. The first weekly newspapers of which we have firm evidence date from 1609; they were printed in the cities of Strasbourg and Wolfenbüttel in Lower Saxony. The exhaustively long title of the Strasbourg publication gives a good indication of what it contained: *Relation of all the best and memorable stories which may betimes unfold and occur in Germany and the Netherlands, also in France,*

Emperor Maximilian I

Maximilian I (1459–1519) was the first emperor to systematically deploy all the benefits of the art of book printing as a tool in how he exercised power. In 1486 at the Imperial Diet in Frankfurt am Main, he was elected King of the Romans, and crowned in Aachen. After the death of his father, Frederick III, in 1493, he acceded to the throne of the Holy Roman Empire and immediately set himself two primary goals: to lead a crusade against the 'unbelievers' and to journey to Rome to be crowned by the Pope. In the event, he was to spend the rest of his life pursuing these in vain. After getting bogged down in conflict several times in northern Italy he eventually had himself proclaimed the 'Elected Roman Emperor' in the cathedral at Trento in February 1508. During his reign a number of measures were implemented that would have far-reaching consequences for the centuries that followed, such as the reform of the empire, the reorganisation of the army and the bureaucracy (at the Diet of Worms in 1495) and the expansion of Habsburg marriage policy to Burgundy, Hungary and Poland (with the founding of the Austro-Hungarian Danube monarchy in 1515). His time on the throne was marked by a constant threat from the Ottoman Turks and Martin Luther's first public hearing at the Diet of Augsburg in 1518, a meeting at which it was decided that Maximilian's successor would be his grandson Charles V (the Fugger banking dynasty of Augsburg was largely instrumental in this choice).

The era of Maximilian saw a marked upswing in artistic and scientific activity, which humanists hailed as the beginning of a golden age. The emperor was receptive to all technological, scientific and artistic innovations and was a great patron both of book printing and of arms manufacture. His interest in printing developed in two directions: first, the publication of pamphlets aimed at swaying public opinion, and, second, the production of extensive laudatory epic works aimed at securing his posthumous fame.

Italy, Scotland and England, Spain, Hungary, Poland, Transylvania, Wallachia, Moldavia, Turkey, etc. in the year 1609. Conveyed and rendered into print with the utmost faithfulness and all the accuracy with which I obtained them. The editor, Johann Carolus of Strasbourg, who published this weekly newspaper in the form of a pamphlet of two sheets and four pages, generally strung the individual articles together without comment. At the same time, the *Aviso* appeared in Wolfenbüttel, printed by Julius Adolf von Söhne. Both works favoured the quarto format, although the *Aviso* had a total of eight pages as against the *Relation*'s four. Two-thirds of the *Aviso*'s articles reported on political events – wars, civil strife, conflicts between social classes and so on – while the rest dealt with business and commerce. The next significant step in the history of the press was the publication of the first daily newspaper – the *Einkommende Zeitungen* ('Tidings Received'), printed in Leipzig from 1650.

Alongside book printing, the printing of newspapers was the second important step in the development of Gutenberg's technology and was one which in particular brought the mass-communication character of his invention to the fore.

A retrospective on the era of Gutenberg

The first books that were printed by Gutenberg imitated manuscripts by adopting their division into columns, their rubrication and their fonts. Only gradually did printing develop its own distinctive traits, such as the title page (which was used to advertise the book), page numbers, an index and so forth. Similarly, to begin with the contents seamlessly followed on from the manuscript era, with the same key theological and scholarly writings that had been the focus of interest in the preceding decades being brought into print. Thereafter, new texts and new literary genres such as prose novels in vernacular languages were to emerge, which utilised the intrinsic potential of the new medium. Extensive reference works, anthologies, legal and theological texts, news about natural catastrophes or war and peace in pamphlets or small tracts all profited from the swift and large-scale reproduction that Gutenberg's invention allowed. The proportion of Latin publications began to decline steadily in favour of vernacular languages, while parchment was wholly supplanted by paper, and the price of books dropped, even after just 30 years, to a quarter of what it had been previously. The educational movement of humanism – which had been associated with the printing press from the outset – and the Reformation promoted the spread of reading, which, in turn, resulted in higher print runs for publications.

Individual elements of Gutenberg's inventions were constantly improved upon: rubrication, more refined metal-cutting techniques, new methods of illustration and smaller-format books gradually

...selves. Even so, the basic principles of the invention ...nchanged – for 350 years. It was only the advent of indus-...on, with the arrival of the first steam-driven rapid press in ...the introduction of paper in rolls and the invention of mecha-...ed typesetting systems (Linotype and Monotype) in the late 19th ...entury, that created new working practices. Innovations in the 20th century, such as photocomposition and offset printing, then moved printing on from the 'hot metal' era and from such high-pressure processes as letterpress. The disbanding of the Federation of Type-setters in 1970 – an event that went largely unnoticed by the general public – symbolically marked the demise of a key technology of the Gutenberg era.

Electronic publishing and digital printing have now largely entirely parted company with the physical aspect of the typographi-cal inventions of the 15th century. In digital printing, electronically typeset content is sent directly from a computer to the printing press with no need for any hard copy along the way. This has facilitated small print runs, print on demand and even personalised prints, since, in principle, every sheet can be printed differently. Because, say, print runs in the academic realm are shrinking markedly, digital printing here ensures that works can still be produced cost-effectively. On the other hand, modern printing techniques such as frequency-modu-lated (FM) screening in offset printing enable the highest quality to be achieved in art books and the like.

The medium of the book is currently experiencing its period of greatest change since Gutenberg's time: after what was initially a somewhat hesitant start to electronic publishing in the 1990s the widespread availability worldwide of cheap and fit-for-purpose e-book readers and tablets to the general public has brought about a fundamental change in the way people consume and respond to books. New experimental business and pricing models have already had a direct effect on the hitherto leading role of brick-and-mortar book retailing, prompting a noticeable shift to online retailers of

Johannes Gutenberg, as portrayed in a larger-than-life-size bust by the sculptor Wäinö Aaltonen, 1962

both printed books and e-books as well as a move away from the classic publishing model to internet providers and self-publishing.

These technological innovations have meant that the classic printed text has been divested of its traditional standalone status and have given rise to a completely new, convergent mode of media behaviour that entails a merging of audio and video and of the moving image and interactive graphics with the printed word. Diverse media now combine to tell a complete story: tie-in books are published on popular film or television series, with accompanying discussions on social networks, with possibly a graphic-novel spin-off, a talk show on the topic or an associated music video. Enhanced e-books are a useful first attempt to combine all these varied technological possibilities within one medium.

Over the following years, it will become clearer what future role and significance the book will have, in its printed and electronic forms respectively, in the transmission of knowledge and learning, entertainment and the dissemination of factual information. It would appear that, much like the paperback in relation to the hardback, the e-book is in the process of finding its own niche, specific to certain requirements and target markets. Easy legibility, an appropriate choice of font and good typography and page design still show a direct line of descent from the first printed book of note in which Gutenberg displayed his mastery of typography. It will be incumbent upon future technical developments not to fall short of the high standards that he set.

However, in terms of cultural history it is vital that the impetus towards education that was prompted by Gutenberg's inventions, including universal free and unimpeded access to knowledge and learning, must be guaranteed in the electronic age, too. The things that we associate with Gutenberg's name are first-class typography, a printing process proven over centuries and the era of mass communication – an era which at present is developing virally thanks to new technological possibilities.

Notes

1   *Korea's Early Printing Culture*, catalogue, Seoul, 1993;
International Symposium on the Printing in East and West,
Seoul, 1997; Po-Kee Sohn: 'Invention of the Movable Metal-
Type Printing in Koryo: Its Role and Impact on Human
Cultural Progress'. In: *Gutenberg-Jahrbuch* 1998, pp. 25–30

2   *Blockbücher des Mittelalters. Bilderfolgen als Lektüre*, catalogue,
published by the Gutenberg Gesellschaft and the Gutenberg
Museum, Mainz, 1991

3   Michael Matheus: 'Vom Bistumsstreit zur Mainzer Stiftsfehde.
Zur Geschichte der Stadt Mainz 1328 bis 1459'. In: *Mainz. Die
Geschichte der Stadt*, ed. by Franz Dumont, Ferdinand Scherf
and Friedrich Schütz, Mainz, 1998, pp. 171–204

4   *Gutenberg-Fest zu Mainz im Jahr 1900*, Mainz, 1901

5   Stadtarchiv Erfurt, Universitätsmatrikel, Signatur 1–16XB
XIII–46, vol. 1, fol. 51 verso, under the rectorship of Johannes
Scheubing (summer semester 1418) and fol. 54 recto under the
rectorship of Henricus de Morle (winter semester 1418–19)

6   Gustav Freiherr von Schenk zu Schweinsberg: 'Genealogie
des Mainzer Geschlechtes Gänsfleisch'. In: *Festschrift zum
fünfhundertjährigen Geburtstage von Johann Gutenberg*, ed. by
Otto Hartwig, Mainz, 1900, pp. 65–130

7   Karl Schorbach: 'Die urkundlichen Nachrichten über
Johann Gutenberg'. In: *Festschrift zum fünfhundertjährigen*

Geburtstage von Johann Gutenberg, ed. by Otto Hartwig, Mainz, 1900, with facsimile supplements, no. II, p. 135 f.

8   Ibid. no. III, p. 137 f.

9   Ibid. no. IV, pp. 138–43

10 Ibid no.VI, p. 145 f.

11 Ibid no. X, pp. 151–4

12 Ibid no. XI, pp. 154–76

13 Wolfgang von Stromer: 'Hans Friedel von Seckingen, der Bankier der Straßburger Gutenberg-Gesellschaften'. In: *Gutenberg-Jahrbuch* 1983, pp. 45–8

14 Stephan Pelgen: 'Zur Archäologie der Buchdrucklettern', In: *Gutenberg-Jahrbuch* 1996, pp. 182–208

15 C.H. Bloy: *A History of Printing Ink, Balls and Rollers 1440–1850*, London, 1967, pp. 1–48

16 Achim Rosenberg, Martin Boghardt, Heiko Dittmann, Dieter Heimermann, Anno Hein, Hans Mommsen: 'Röntgenfluoreszenzanalyse der Druckerschwärzen des Mainzer *Catholicon* und anderer Frühdrucke mit Synchrotonstrahlung'. In: *Gutenberg-Jahrbuch* 1998, pp. 231–55

17 Cf. E. Vaassen: 'Zur Mainzer Riesenbibel'. In: *Archiv für Geschichte des Buchwesens* 13, 1973, pp. 1121–8

18 Alfred Swierk: 'Johannes Gutenberg als Erfinder in Zeugnissen seiner Zeit'. In: Hans Widmann (ed.): *Der gegenwärtige Stand der Gutenberg-Forschung*, Stuttgart, 1972, no. 14, p. 86 f.

19 Severin Corsten: 'Die Drucklegung der zweiundvierzigzeiligen Bibel. Technische und chronologische Probleme'. In: *Johannes Gutenbergs zweiundvierzigzeilige Bibel. Faksimile-Ausgabe nach dem Exemplar der Staatsbibliothek Preußischer Kulturbesitz Berlin. Kommentarband*, ed. by Wieland Schmidt, Munich, 1979, pp. 33–68

20 'Faksimile (nach dem Exemplar der Bayerischen Staatsbibliothek, Cim. 63 a) mit Kommentar bei Wieland

Schmidt: Zur Tabula Rubricarum'. In: *Faksimile Berlin* 1979, commentary, pp. 177–83

21 Corsten: *Drucklegung*, p. 51 f.

22 R.N. Schwab: 'Cyclotron Analyses of the Ink in the 42-line Bible'. In: *The Papers of the Bibliographical Society of America* 77, 1983, pp. 285–315

23 Hans-Michael Empell: *Gutenberg vor Gericht. Der Mainzer Prozess um die erste gedruckte Bibel*, Frankfurt am Main and elsewhere, 2008 (= Rechtshistorische Reihe, vol. 372)

24 Vellum MS from Mainz dated 5 November 1455, from the State and University Library, Göttingen (SuUB Göttingen), Sign.: 2° Code. MS. Hist. lit. 123 Cim.

25 Empell: *Gutenberg vor Gericht*, p. 150

26 Tatiana Dolgodrova: 'Die Miniaturen der Leipziger Pergament-Ausgabe der Gutenberg-Bibel – zur Zeit in der Russischen Staatsbibliothek, Moskau – ein hervorragendes Denkmal der Buchkunst'. In: GJ 72, 1997, pp. 64–75; Leonhard Hoffmann: 'Wann hat Johannes Gutenberg die zweiundvierzigzeilige Bibel gedruckt? Ein Datierungsversuch nach Äußerungen von Zeitzeugen'. In: *Archiv für Geschichte des Buchwesens*, vol. 58, 2004, pp. 211–20

27 SuUB Göttingen, Sign.: 2° Bibl. I, 5955 Inc. Rara Cim. Handwritten marginalia indicate that this outstanding copy once belonged to a monastery. In 1587 it came into the possession of Duke Julius of Brunswick (founder of the Herzog August Library in Wolfenbüttel), and in 1614, along with the rest of the older Wolfenbüttel Library, it went to the University Library of Helmstedt. After the dissolution of the University of Helmstedt the Bible came to Göttingen in 1812, where it has remained ever since.

28 Vellum MS, *c.* 1450. Ex.: SuUB Göttingen, Sign.: 8° Cod. MS. Uff. 51 Cim.

29 The copy of the letter of indulgence illustrated, from the State and University Library Göttingen (GW 6556), was issued on 26 January 1455, Sign.: 2° Hist. lit. libr. I, 751 no. 10

30 Kai Michael Sprenger: '"Volumus tamen, quod expressio fiat ante finem mensis Maii presentis". Sollte Gutenberg 1452 im Auftrag Nikolaus' von Kues Ablaßbriefe drucken?' In: *Gutenberg-Jahrbuch* 1999, pp. 42–57

31 *Der Türkenkalender*, facsimile ed. by Ferdinand Geldner, Wiesbaden, 1975

32 Aloys Ruppel: *Johannes Gutenberg: Sein Leben und sein Werk. Nachdruck der zweiten Auflage*, Berlin, 1939 (new editions 1947 and 1967), p. 127, illustration of the title page in Albert Kapr: *Johannes Gutenberg. Persönlichkeit und Leistung*, 2nd edn, Munich, 1988, p. 214

33 Illustration in Kapr: *Gutenberg*, p. 215

34 See Holger Nickel: 'Handschrift und Druck im 15. Jahrhundert: Zwolle'. In: *Quärendo* 41, 2011, pp. 351–9; Nickel provides comparative figures for the distribution of schoolbooks throughout the whole of Europe.

35 Hans Widmann: *Der deutsche Buchhandel in Urkunden und Quellen, Vol. 1*, Hamburg, 1965, p. 16 f.

36 Paul Needham: 'Johann Gutenberg and the Catholicon Press'. In: *The Papers of the Bibliographical Society of America* 76, 1982 , pp. 395–456; for an alternative view, cf. Lotte Hellinga: 'Das Mainzer Catholicon und Gutenbergs Nachlaß: Neudatierungen und Auswirkungen'. In: *Archiv für Geschichte des Buchwesens* 40, 1993, pp. 395–416

37 Schorbach: 'Urkundliche Nachrichten', no. XXVII, pp. 227–33

38 Michael Mommert: 'Konrad Humery und seine Übersetzung der "Consolatio philosophiae"'. Diss. phil., Münster, 1965; Franz-Josef Worstbrock: 'Konrad Humery'. In: *Die deutsche Literatur des Mittelalters. Verfasserlexikon*. vol. 4. Berlin, New York, 1983, cols. 301–4

39 Schorbach: 'Urkundliche Nachrichten', no. XXV, p. 220 f.,
    plate 22

40 Klaus Grubmüller: *Vocabularius ex quo. Untersuchungen zu
    lateinisch-deutschen Vokabularien des Spätmittelalters*, Munich,
    1967 (*Münchener Texte und Untersuchungen zur deutschen
    Literatur des Mittelalters*, vol. 17)

41 Useful and accurate information about printing in Eltville can
    be found in Hans Widmann: *Eltvilles Anteil am Frühdruck.
    Tatsachen und Probleme*, Eltville, 1970, p. 18

42 George D. Painter: 'The Untrue portraits of Johann
    Gutenberg. With six figures'. In: *Gutenberg-Jahrbuch* 1967, pp.
    54–60

43 Basle, Nikolaus Brylinger, 3 vols, illustration in vol. 2, p. 397

44 Heinrich Pantaleon: *Teutscher Nation Heldenbuch*, Basle,
    Nikolaus Brylinger, vol. 2, 1568, p. 507; the same woodcut
    appears in vol. 1, p. 59, purportedly showing Othonius, the
    necromancer, as well as in vol. 2, p. 30, Irmenreich, the apostle
    to the Bulgars, and elsewhere.

45 André Thevet: *Les Vrais pourtraits et vies des hommes illustres*,
    Paris, 1584, fol. 514 recto

46 Severin Corsten: 'Von Bernhard von Mallinckrodt
    zu Ludwig Hain. Ziele und Methoden der frühen
    Inkunabelbibliographie'. In: *Gutenberg-Jahrbuch* 1995, pp.
    37–50

47 Stephan Füssel (ed.): *Im Zentrum: das Buch. 50 Jahre
    Buchwissenschaft in Mainz*, Mainz, 1997 (Kleiner Druck no.
    112)

48 Facsimile in Widmann: *Der deutsche Buchhandel*, p. 17

49 Otto Mazal: *Der Mainzer Psalter von 1457. Kommentar zum
    Faksimiledruck von 1457*, Zürich, 1969, p. 80 ff.: Die Initialen

50 Arnold Esch: 'Deutsche Frühdrucker in Rom in den Registern
    Papst Pauls II'. In: *Gutenberg-Jahrbuch* 1993, pp. 44–52

51 Ibid. p. 48

52 This section about the book in Britain is from: Stephan
    Füssel: *Gutenberg and the impact of printing*, trans. by Douglas
    Martin, Scholar Press, Ashgate Publishing Ltd, Aldershot,
    Hampshire, 2005, pp. 66–70

53 Stephan Füssel: '"Dem Drucker aber sage er Dank ..." Zur
    wechselseitigen Bereicherung von Buchdruckerkunst und
    Humanismus'. In: *Artibus. Kulturwissenschaft und deutsche
    Philologie des Mittelalters und der frühen Neuzeit*, ed. by
    Stephan Füssel, Gert Hübner and Joachim Knape, Wiesbaden,
    1994, pp. 167–78

54 Peter F. Tschudin: 'Erasmus und der Buchdruck'. In: *Erasmus
    von Rotterdam. Katalog zur Ausstellung zum 450. Todestag
    [catalogue of the exhibition marking the 450th anniversary of
    Erasmus' death] im Historischen Museum Basel, Basle, 1986,
    pp. 41–8

Testimonies

Enea Silvio Piccolomini (later Pope Pius II)
What was written to me about that marvellous man in Frankfurt was undoubtedly true. I have not seen complete copies of his Bible, but I did see a number of quinternions [bound signatures of five folded sheets] of various books [of the Bible], executed in a very neat and legible script, which Your Grace would be able to read without the slightest trouble and indeed with no need even to use your glasses. Several people told me that 158 copies have been finished, although others say there are 180. I am not certain of the exact number, but I'm in no doubt that the volumes are complete, if my informants are to be trusted. Had I known your wishes I should certainly have bought you a copy – some quinternions were actually brought here to the emperor. If I can I will try and get one of the Bibles that are for sale brought here, which I can then purchase on your behalf, but I fear that might not be possible, both because of the length of the journey and because buyers are apparently already lining up to buy the copies even before they are finished.

Letter of 12 March 1455 from Wiener Neustadt
to Cardinal Juan de Carvajal

Franciscus Philelpus
I have decided to purchase a number of those books that are now being created without any effort or writing materials but rather by means of certain 'forms', as the technical expression goes. These are so

accomplished that one might well believe that they had come from the hand of the most skilled copyist.

Milan, 1470

Guillaume Fichet

As far as I can tell, a great light has been shed upon the sciences by a new species of scribe whom Germany (like some latter-day Trojan horse) has been pouring forth in every direction. For in that land, not far from the city of Mainz, there was a certain Johann who bore the surname Gutenberg [bonnemontanus], who was the first man to devise the art of printing, whereby books are made not written with a reed (as the ancients did), nor with a quill pen (as we do nowadays), but with metal letters, and, moreover, with great speed, elegance and beauty. Surely this man deserves to have divine praises heaped upon him by all the Muses, by all branches of learning and by all those who delight in books.

Letter to Robert Gaguin, Paris, some time after 1 January 1471

Nicolaus Perotus

I have frequently had occasion to marvel at the good fortune of our generation in having had such a truly great and divine blessing bestowed upon us in our lifetime, in the form of the new mode of reproduction that has recently come to us from Germany. For I have seen with my own eyes how it is now possible for a single person to print, within a month, as many – if not more – tracts than he would have struggled to produce even over an entire year. Accordingly, I hope within a short space of time to see such a great multitude of books appear that even the poor and indigent will not need in future to forego reading any volume they choose.

Ulm, 1471

Bonus Accursivus

I'm sure you are aware that the by-now familiar art of book printing first appeared in our time. It is a truly beneficial and even beautiful art form, since it has hitherto not exactly been easy for all people to acquire handwritten copies of books, because of their high price. But even in the event that you – by God's good grace – should find cost no impediment, you must surely still admire book printing for its artistic beauty and also for the fact that the printed word, once properly set, then proceeds to appear in identical form on each and every sheet, with the result that errors are virtually impossible, quite unlike the business of transcribing by hand.

Milan, 1475

Censorship edict issued by Berthold von Henneberg, Archbishop-Elector of Mainz

While it is true that the so-called divine art of printing has enabled people to get hold of books readily from various different disciplines in ample quantities and to use them to gain scholarly knowledge, we have none the less had cause to note that certain people, seduced by a vain desire for fame and money, have abused this art and in so doing sent something that was intended to make our lives more cultivated down the path of perdition and corruption. For we have seen how books which contain the order of the Sacred Mass and discuss divine matters and the key questions of our faith have been translated from the Latin into the German language and freely distributed among the general populace, much to the detriment of religion. [...] Who will enable laymen and uneducated people and the female sex, once they have the books of Holy Scripture in their hands, to discover their true meaning? [...] And so we decree that no works of whatever kind, no matter to which science, art or other branch of learning they relate, should be translated from the Greek, Latin or another language into the German vernacular [...] Nor are they to be disseminated or purchased, either publicly or clandestinely, directly or indirectly, unless the works proposed for printing have first been scrutinised before they go to press and officially authorised for publication by specially appointed doctors and masters of our university in our city of Mainz.

22 March 1485

Peter Danhauser

How cheaply one can come by the treasures of classical learning nowadays. They have been hauled out from the most hidden corners of libraries where they once resided [...] and works which formerly only kings and princes could afford are now within reach of even a poor man. Accordingly [...] anyone who aspires to lead a moral life and to become a good philosopher should purchase this book, while at the same time thanking the printer for furnishing him with such a useful gift.

Epigram in the work Repertorium auctoritatum Aristotelis et aliorum
philosophorum, attributed to the Venerable Bede, Nuremberg, 1491

Hartmann Schedel

The art of printing was first developed on German territory, in the city of Mainz on the Rhine, in the year of our Lord 1440, and spread from there to almost all parts of the world. Through it, the precious treasures of the written word and the wisdom contained in the books of the ancients – which languished for a long time, hidden and unknown, in the grave of ignorance – have been brought to light [...] If this art had been invented and put into use earlier, then no doubt many books by Livy, Cicero or Pliny and other highly learned people would not have fallen into desuetude for centuries. And while no little praise is due to the original inventors of manual book printing, how inexpressibly greater is the acclaim, praise, honour and glory owing to the Germans, whose enlightened, inventive and skilled know-how enabled them to devise this form of mechanical printing. For it has opened up to the common man the long-sealed wellspring of profound knowledge of both the human and the divine arts.

Nuremberg Chronicle, 1493, fol. 252 verso

Sebastian Brant

Recently a combination of intellect and artistry has brought forth a considerable number of books from the Rhineland. A book – a possession that only wealthy men and the king could once call their own – can now be found in even the humblest of homes. Thanks be to the gods, first and foremost, but also to the printers, whose unceasing efforts have allowed them to master this art. This new invention, which eluded both the scholars of ancient Greece and the engineers of Rome, is a product of German ingenuity.

'Poem on the Excellence of the Printer's Art', Basle, 1498

Cologne Chronicle

On the art of book printing: when, where and by whom the ineffably useful art of printing books was invented. This invaluable skill was first invented in Germany, at Mainz on the Rhine, and it is a great credit to the German nation that such ingenious men are to be found there. This event took place in the year of our Lord 1440, and from that time until 1450 the art, and everything associated with it, was the subject of further development. And in the year of our Lord 1450, which was a golden year [jubilee], actual printing began, and the first book to be printed was a Latin Bible; it was printed in a large typeface that is otherwise used in missals. [...] The first inventor of book printing was a citizen of Mainz, Squire Johannes Gutenberg by name.

Cologne, 1499

Polydorus Vergilius

Our age has witnessed the invention of a new form of writing. Now, in a single day, one person can print more text than several scribes were able to produce by hand in a whole year. As a result we have suddenly come by such a great quantity of books in all fields of learning that a person need scarcely want for any book, be he ever so impecunious. In addition, the invention of printing has saved a great number of Greek and Latin authors from being lost for all time. Therefore, we should be unstinting in our acclaim of the man who devised such an important invention, above all in order that later generations might know whom they have to thank for this piece of divine beneficence. This art of printing texts was invented by Johann Gutenberg, a native of the German nation and a man of knightly standing, in Mainz on the Rhine.

Polydori Vergilii Urbinatis de inventoribus rerum libri tres, Venice, 1499, fol. 5

Joachim Vadian

The German who cast letters from metal and who clearly demonstrated that a single printing process was easily capable of competing with the best daily output of even the swiftest of scribes, has at a stroke outshone all the inventions of the ancient world. May all blessings and boundless good fortune be upon him.

In arte impressoriae meritem laudem, 1511

Johannes Trithemius

At that time the German city of Mainz on the Rhine – and not Italy, as has sometimes been incorrectly claimed – saw the invention and development of that splendid and hitherto unknown art of printing by Johannes Gutenberg, a citizen of Mainz. He invested almost his entire fortune in this enterprise. Yet after having failed to get this or that technique to work properly and finding himself thwarted by insurmountable problems, he was on the point of abandoning the entire undertaking in despair when his fellow citizen Johann Fust stepped in to offer his advice and his financial support, enabling him to successfully complete the work he had begun.

Annales Hirsaugiensis, 1515

Martin Luther

Printing is the greatest and ultimate gift, through which God wants the whole world, to the ends of the earth, to know the roots of true religion and to broadcast it in every language. Printing is the last flicker of the flame that glows before the extinction of this world.

Johannes Aurifaber: *Tischreden oder Colloquia Doctor Martin Luthers*, Frankfurt am Main, 1566

Johann Wolfgang von Goethe
Printing and the freedom this has promoted have been of immense use and brought us incalculable benefits.

Dichtung und Wahrheit, 1812

The art of printing is an established fact marking the start of a second phase in the history of the world and art – a phase that is utterly different from the one that went before.

1820

Victor Hugo
In the 15th century everything changes. Human thought discovers a mode of perpetuating itself, not only more durable and more resisting than architecture, but still more simple and easy. Architecture is dethroned. Gutenberg's letters of lead are about to supersede Orpheus' letters of stone. [...] The invention of printing is the greatest event in history. It is the mother of revolution. It is the mode of expression of humanity which is totally renewed [...] In its printed form thought is more imperishable than ever; it is volatile, irresistible, indestructible. [...] Now it converts itself into a flock of birds, scatters itself to the four winds and occupies all points of air and space at once.

Notre-Dame de Paris, 1831

Mark Twain
The world concedes without hesitation or dispute that Gutenberg's invention is incomparably the mightiest event that has ever

happened in profane history. It created a new and wonderful earth, and along with it a new hell. [...] Whatever the world is, today, good and bad together, that is what Gutenberg's invention has made it: for from that source it has all come. But he has our homage; for what he said to the reproaching angel in his dream has come true, and the evil wrought through his mighty invention is immeasurably outbalanced by the good it has brought to the race of men.

From a letter of 7 April 1900 sent from London to Adolf Goerz, the driving force behind the founding of the Gutenberg Museum

John Updike

GUTENBERG (*hesitantly*): Perhaps the book, like God, is an idea some men will cling to. [...] This electronic flood you describe has no banks; it massively delivers, but what, to whom? There is something intrinsically small about its content, compared with the genius of its workings. [...] You speak of this global Internet as if it transcended human brains; but man is still the measure of all things.

BILL GATES (*collapsing with a hiss*): Oh? Who sayssss?

'Dialogue in Cyberspace': Lufthansa inflight magazine 5/1995

The rationale for Gutenberg's ranking as the 'Man of the Millennium'

If not for Gutenberg, Columbus [ranked no. 2] might never have set sail, Shakespeare's genius [no. 5] could have died with him, and Martin Luther's *Ninety-five Theses* [no. 3] would have hung on that door unheeded. [...] The printing press, developed by goldsmith Gutenberg in the 1430s, helped spread truth, beauty and, yes, heresy throughout the world. [...] Copies of his first major project, the Bible, survive today. He worked for years to perfect his system of movable type and a press that could mass-produce books, leaflets and propaganda. What little is known about Gutenberg comes from the many lawsuits filed against him for rights to the invention. But no one successfully challenged Gutenberg's place as the Western inventor of movable type and the printing press. Because his press unharnessed the power of ideas on the world, we rank him ahead of the people whose ideas found an audience through printing.

Agnes Hooper Gottlieb, Henry Gottlieb, Barbara Bowers, Brent Bowers: *1000 Years, 1000 People: Ranking the Men and Women Who Shaped the Millennium*. New York, Tokyo, London, 1999, p. 2

Surviving Gutenberg Bibles

Austria
Vienna, Österreichische Nationalbibliothek 2 vols*

Belgium
Mons, Bibliothèque Municipale vol. 1

Denmark
Copenhagen, Kongelige Bibliotek vol. 2

France
Paris, Bibliothèque Mazarine 2 vols*
Paris, Bibliothèque Nationale 2 vols
Paris, Bibliothèque Nationale 2 vols vellum*
Saint-Omer, Bibliothèque Municipale vol. 1

Germany
Aschaffenburg, Hofbibliothek 2 vols
Berlin, Staatsbibliothek 2 vols vellum
Frankfurt am Main, Universitätsbibliothek Johann Christian
    Senckenberg 2 vols*
Fulda, Hochschul- und Landesbibliothek vol. 1 vellum
Göttingen, Niedersächsische Staats- und Universitätsbibliothek 2
    vols vellum*
Kassel, Murhardsche Bibliothek vol. 1

Leipzig, Universitätsbibliothek 4 vols vellum
Mainz, Gutenberg-Museum 2 vols
Mainz, Gutenberg-Museum vol. 2
Munich, Bayerische Staatsbibliothek 2 vols*
Schleswig, Landesmuseum für Kunst- und Kulturgeschichte
     Schloss Gottorf vol. 1
Schweinfurt, Bibliothek Otto Schäfer 2 vols
Stuttgart, Württembergische Landesbibliothek 2 vols
Trier, Stadtbibliothek Weberbach vol. 1

Great Britain
Cambridge, University Library 2 vols*
Edinburgh, National Library 2 vols*
Eton, College Library 2 vols*
London, British Library 2 vols*
London, British Library 2 vols vellum*
London, Archiepiscopal Library, Lambeth Palace vol. 2 (NT only)
     vellum
Manchester, John Rylands Library 2 vols*
Oxford, Bodleian Library 2 vols*

Japan
Tokyo, Keio University vol. 1

Poland
Pelplin, Biblioteka Seminarium Duchownego 2 vols

Portugal
Lisbon, Biblioteca Nacional e Instituto do Livro 2 vols

Russia
Moscow, State Library + 2 vols vellum
Moscow, Lomonosow University Library ++ 2 vols

Spain
Burgos, Biblioteca Pública del Estado 2 vols
Seville, Biblioteca Universitaria y Provincial vol. 2 (NT only)

Switzerland
Cologny, Bibliotheca Bodmeriana 2 vols

USA
Austin, Texas, Harry Ransom Humanities Research Center 2 vols*
Cambridge, Massachusetts, Harry Elkins Widener Memorial
    Library 2 vols*
New Haven, Connecticut, Beinecke Rare Book and Manuscript
    Library 2 vols*
New York, Pierpont Morgan Library 2 vols*
New York, Pierpont Morgan Library 2 vols vellum
New York, Pierpont Morgan Library vol. 1
New York, Public Library 2 vols
Princeton, John H. Scheide Library 2 vols
San Marino, California, Henry H. Huntington Library 2 vols vellum
Washington, DC, Library of Congress 3 vols vellum*

Vatican
Roma, Biblioteca Apostolica Vaticana 2 vols
Roma, Biblioteca Apostolica Vaticana / Barberini 2 vols vellum

The locations given are those of B 42, GW 4201 and H 3083
The Bibles were normally bound in two volumes; one exception to this is the
    copy held by the Library of Congress, Washington, DC, which was bound
    in three volumes.
* = complete
NT = New Testament
+ = from the holdings of the German Book and Manuscript Museum, Leipzig
++ = from the holdings of Leipzig University Library

List of digital editions of the Gutenberg Bible available on the internet

Location	Web address
Austria	
Österreichische Nationalbibliothek, Vienna	http://data.onb.ac.at/dtl/2176396
France	
Bibliothèque Mazarine, Paris	http://mazarinum.bibliotheque-mazarine.fr/idurl/1/1703 (in French)
Bibliothèque Nationale, Paris (vellum copy)	http://gallica.bnf.fr/ark:/12148/bpt6k9912811
Bibliothèque Nationale, Paris (paper copy)	http://gallica.bnf.fr/ark:/12148/bpt6k991433p
Bibliothèque Municipale, Saint-Omer	http://bibliotheque-numerique.bibliotheque-agglo-stomer.fr/idurl/1/1905 (in French)
Germany	
Staatsbibliothek, Berlin	http://resolver.staatsbibliothek-berlin.de/SBB0001E0ED00000000

Location	Web address
Universitätsbibliothek, Frankfurt am Main	http://nbn-resolving.de/urn:nbn:de:hebis:30:2-13096
Hochschul- und Landesbibliothek, Fulda	http://fuldig.hs-fulda.de/viewer/resolver?urn=urn%3Anbn%3Ade%3Ahebis%3A66%3Afuldig-6273288
SUB, Göttingen	http://gutenbergdigital.de/
Bayerische Staatsbibliothek, Munich	Vol. 1: http://daten.digitale-sammlungen.de/~db/bsb00004647/images/ Vol. 2: http://daten.digitale-sammlungen.de/~db/bsb00004648/images/
Württemburg Landesbibliothek, Stuttgart	http://digital.wlb-stuttgart.de/purl/bsz348625510

Great Britain

Cambridge University	http://cudl.lib.cam.ac.uk/view/PR-INC-00001-A-00001-00001-03761/1
National Library, Edinburgh	http://digital.nls.uk/74481666
British Library, London	http://molcat1.bl.uk/treasures/gutenberg/homepage.html
John Rylands Library, Manchester	http://johannes.library.manchester.ac.uk:8181/luna/servlet/detail/
Bodleian Library, Oxford	Vol. 1: http://digital.bodleian.ox.ac.uk/inquire/p/04d9da19-eec2-4a0a-8287-749f554540cd Vol. 2: http://digital.bodleian.ox.ac.uk/inquire/p/7a0da94e-3590-4a1a-8852-3c25ca4f5e93

Location	Web address
Japan	
Keio University, Tokyo	http://dcollections.lib.keio.ac.jp/ja/gutenberg (In Japanese)
Spain	
Biblioteca Pública del Estado, Burgos	http://bvpb.mcu.es/es/consulta/registro.cmd?id=485858 (in Spanish)
Biblioteca de la Universidad de Sevilla, Seville	http://fondosdigitales.us.es/fondos/libros/9070/1/biblia-latin/
USA	
Harry Ransom Center, University of Texas	http://www.hrc.utexas.edu/exhibitions/permanent/gutenbergbible/
Harry Elkins Widener Memorial Library, Cambridge, Massachusetts	Vol. 1: http://nrs.harvard.edu/urn-3:FHCL.HOUGH:5339979 Vol. 2: http://nrs.harvard.edu/urn-3:FHCL.HOUGH:1140421
Morgan Library, New York (OT)	http://www.themorgan.org/collections/works/gutenberg/page/1
Library of Congress, Washington, DC	http://rarebookroom.org/Control/gtnbbl/index.html
John H. Scheide Library, Princeton	http://arks.princeton.edu/ark:/88435/7d278t10z
Lilly Library, Indiana University (NT)	http://purl.dlib.indiana.edu/iudl/general/VAB8631

Location	Web address
Vatican City	
Biblioteca Apostolica Vaticana, Barberini (vellum copy)	http://digi.vatlib.it/view/Stamp.Barb.AAA.IV.16 http://digi.vatlib.it/view/Stamp.Barb.AAA.IV.17

Notable printers

Johannes Gutenberg	Mainz	*c.* 1400–1468
Johannes Mentelin	Strasbourg	*c.* 1410–1478
Nicolas Jenson	Venice	1420–1480
William Caxton	London	*c.* 1415/22–1492
Günther Zainer	Augsburg	*c.* 1425–1478
Peter Schöffer the Elder	Mainz	*c.* 1430–1502/1503
Johann Amerbach	Basle	1443/45–1513
Anton Koberger	Nuremberg	*c.* 1440–1513
Johann Zainer	Ulm	*c.* 1445–1493
Erhard Ratdolt	Augsburg/Venice	1447–1527/28
Aldus Manutius	Venice	1449–1515
Lucantonio Giunta	Venice	1457–1538
Johann Froben	Basle	*c.* 1460–1527
Geoffroy Tory	Paris	*c.* 1480–1533
Christoph Froschauer the Elder	Zurich	*c.* 1490–1564
Hans Lufft	Wittenberg	1495–1584
Christian Egenolff the Elder	Frankfurt	1502–1555
Robert Stephanus (Etienne)	Paris	1503–1559
Johannes Oporinus	Basle	1507–1568
Christoph Plantin	Antwerp	*c.* 1520–1589
Willem Janszon Blaeu	Amsterdam	1570–1638
Abraham Elzevier	Leiden	1592–1652

Joseph Moxon	London	1627–1691
Johann Gottlob Breitkopf	Leipzig	1719–1794
John Baskerville	Birmingham	1706–1775
Karl Christoph Tauchnitz	Leipzig	1761–1836
Joaquín Ibarra	Madrid	1725–1785
Giambattista Bodoni	Parma	1740–1813
Johann Friedrich Unger	Berlin	1753–1804
Pierre Didot	Paris	1761–1853
William Morris	London	1834–1896
T.J. Cobden-Sanderson	London	1840–1922
Daniel Berkeley Updike	Boston	1860–1941
Frederic Goudy	Chicago	1865–1947
Carl Ernst Poeschel	Berlin	1874–1944
Christian Heinrich Kleukens	Darmstadt	1880–1954
Giovanni (Hans) Mardersteig	Verona	1892–1977

The spread of Gutenberg's technology

c. 1450 Mainz
c. 1460 Bamberg
c. 1460 Strasbourg
1465 Subiaco near
  Rome
1466 Cologne
1467 Eltville
1467 Rome
1468 Augsburg
c. 1468 Basle
1469 Venice
c. 1470 Naples
1470 Nuremberg
1470 Paris
1471 Speyer
1471 Florence
1471 Milan
1473 Esslingen
1473 Lyons
1473 Ulm
1473 Utrecht
1473 Buda
  (Budapest)

c. 1474 Valencia
c. 1474 Lübeck
1474 Bruges
1474 Louvain
1475 Cracow
1475 Wrocław
1475 Zaragoza
1475 Brussels
c. 1476 Westminster,
  London
1476 Plzeň
1479 Würzburg
1480 Leipzig
1480 London
1480 Magdeburg
1481 Antwerp
1481 Salamanca
1482 Odense
1482 Vienna
1483 Stockholm
1487 Prague
1489 Lisbon

1491 Kosinj
  (Croatia)
1493 Copenhagen
1503 Istanbul
c. 1515 Thessaloniki
c. 1553 Moscow
1556 Goa (India)
1583 Lima (Peru)
c. 1590 Kasuza
  (Japan)
1638 Cambridge,
  Massachusetts
  (USA)
c. 1640 Isfahan (Iran)
1706 Recife (Brazil)
1752 Halifax
  (Canada)
1795 Cape Town
1796 Sydney
1798 Cairo
c. 1830 San José
  (Costa Rica)

Notable early printing sites

Stockholm
1483

North Sea

Odense
1482

Copenhagen
1493

Baltic Sea

Lübeck
1475

Rostock
1476

Gdańsk
1498

Malbork
1492

Hamburg
1491

c.1476
Westminster

London
1480

Utrecht 1473

1474
Bruges

Antwerp 1481

Magdeburg 1480

English Channel

Brussels
1475

Louvain
1474

Cologne
1466

Leipzig 1481

Wrocław
1475

Paris
1470

Eltville
1467

Mainz
c.1450

c.1460
Bamberg

Prague 1488

Cracow
1475

Plzeň 1476

Speyer 1476

Nuremburg 1470

Strasbourg
c.1460

Esslingen 1473

Basle
1468

Ulm
1473

Augsburg
1468

Vienna
1482

Buda
1481

Lyons
1473

Milan
1471

Venice
1469

Zaragoza
1475

Florence
1471

Barcelona
1475

Subiaco
1465

Rome
1467

Valencia
1474

Naples
1470

Mediterranean Sea

Key inventions in printing

1st/2nd century AD Paper in widespread use in China.

8th century Woodblock printing in Korea, China and Japan; *The Great Dharani Sutra* is the oldest woodblock print in the world.

11th century Individual characters (movable type) first made from pottery/clay in China.

before 1150 Paper produced in Spain.

before 1230 Paper produced in Italy.

13th century Individual characters cast from metal in Korea.

1348 Construction of a paper mill in the French city of Troyes.

1377 In Korea, movable metal type is used for printing *Jikji*, the world's oldest book to be produced by this method.

1390 The Stromer paper mill is established at Nuremberg, Germany.

1423 The oldest dated woodcut in Europe.

1446 The first verifiable dated copperplate engraving.

1450 Invention of the art of book printing with movable type on a mechanical press by Johannes Gutenberg.

1476 In Rome, Ulrich Han issues the first dated printed book (*Missale Romanum*) containing musical notes.

1502 Ottaviano dei Petrucci of Venice devises a method of printing sheet music, using staves, musical notation and accompanying song text.

1642 Ludwig von Siegen invents the printmaking technique of mezzotint.

1768 The aquatint is invented by Jean Baptiste Le Prince.

1772 In Basle, Switzerland, Wilhelm Haas manufactures an improved hand-operated printing press by adding numerous metal parts.

1783/4 Englishman Thomas Bell patents a technique for printing using a rotogravure forme as well as the use of squeegees in printing.

1796 Aloys Senefelder invents lithography.

1799 Louis-Nicolas Robert patents the first machine to produce 'continuous paper'.

1811 In London, Friedrich Koenig and his co-inventor Andreas Friedrich Bauer unveil the world's first high-speed steam-powered cylinder printing press.

1814 Koenig and Bauer further develop their face-and-back printing press. *The Times* is printed on this type of press from this date.

1819 Jacob Perkins patents the technique of steel engraving.

1820 Invention of a reliable method of paper stereotyping by Jean Baptiste Genoux, a printer from Lyons, France.

1822 A patent for a typesetting machine is granted to William Church of New York.

1838 Moritz Hermann von Jacobi discovers galvanoplastics, a method of making printing plates by electroplating.

1840 Austrian copperplate engraver Blasius Höfel invents line etching.

1851 Appearance of the first platen jobbing presses.

1852 Beginnings of photolithography.

1860 Scottish physicist James Clerk Maxwell demonstrates the first photographic colour-separation procedure, subsequently used in four-colour process printing.

1862 The complete typecasting machine is invented in England.

1865 American William Bullock produces a rotary press that can print on a roll of paper.

1868 Josef Albert develops the first commercially successful collotype process.

1879 Karl Klietsch invents heliogravure.

1881 Printmaker Georg Meisenbach introduces the halftone reprographic process.

1884 Ottmar Mergenthaler perfects a device for casting and setting whole lines ('slugs') of type: the Linotype machine.

1888 The typograph, another matrix-composing and slug-casting machine, is invented in the USA by John Raphael Rogers.

1892 Ernst Vogel and the German–American photographer William Kurtz develop halftone colour printing.

1894 Eugene Porzolt undertakes the first experiments in photocomposition, a photographic method for composing type based on letters projected on to a light-sensitive plate.

1897 In the USA Tolbert Lanston constructs the first Monotype machine.

1903/4 Ira W. Rubel and Caspar Hermann develop offset printing independently of one another.

1914 The first flexographic printing machine is put on the market by the firm Windmöller & Hölscher of Lengerich, Germany.

1914 The first fully automatic platen press is developed by the Heidelberger Druckmaschinen company in Germany.

1924 The first screen-printing machine is made by the firm Selectasine in the USA.

1927 Hungarian inventor Edmund Uher develops one of the first successful phototypesetting machines, the Uhertype.

1936 First use of halftone gravure printing.

1937 American physicist Chester F. Carlson pioneers xerography, a dry photocopying process.

1940 Invention of the anilox roller for flexographic printing in the USA.

1948 First large-scale application of phototypesetting using the photosetter.

1949 Introduction by the US Photon company of the first electromechanical photocomposition system, the Lumitype.

1950 First use of a punched-tape control system on the Linotype TTS (TeleTypeSetter).

1950 Aluminium plates are introduced in offset printing.

1953 Rudolf Hell invents the Klischograph, an electromechanical engraving machine for the production of high-pressure (letterpress) halftone printing plates (clichés).

1962 The Hell company develops the Helio-Klischograph, designed for engraving gravure cylinders, and the Chromograph, a colour scanner that produces four-colour separation.

1970 Trialling of the first electronic phototypesetting systems.

1970 Introduction of photopolymer plates in high-pressure print systems (letterpress and flexography).

1972 The dry-offset process (also known as indirect letterpress) is invented.

1975 Cathode-ray exposure in photocomposition.

1980s Development of computer-to-plate /computer-to-cylinder technology.

1983 Gerhard Fischer invents frequency-modulated (FM) screening.

1984 The PostScript page-description language, developed by Adobe, ushers in the desktop publishing revolution. Introduction of the laser scanner in phototypesetting.

1984/5 Advent of the era of desktop publishing, in which text and images are created using page layout software on personal computers. The first viable page make-up program is PageMaker, developed by Aldus and later bought by Adobe.

1987 Introduction of QuarkXPress page make-up software, formerly an industry-standard program that is still in use today.

1990 The image-editing program Photoshop, still in widespread use today, is introduced by Adobe.

1990 The company Komori introduces the automatic plate-changer on offset printing presses.

1990s Introduction of anilox inking units on flexo and offset rotary printing presses.

1992 Introduction of computer-to-press technology.

1993 The firms Indigo and Xeikon unveil their first digital printers, which are based on xerography technology. Adobe introduces its file format PDF (Portable Document Format) for text formatting and images, based on its PostScript language. PDFs remain a highly popular method of data transfer.

1995 The Quickmaster DI (QMDI), manufactured by Heidelberger Druckmaschinen, becomes the first freestanding computer-to-press offset press to appear on the market.

1996 The Swiss company Dätwyler devises a viable laser engraving process for gravure cylinders.

late 1990s Large-format printing (LFP) by inkjet becomes widespread. OpenType printer fonts are developed by Adobe and Microsoft.

1999 Adobe unveils the page-make-up program InDesign, still widely used by designers and typesetters.

2000 Joseph Jacobson of MIT, USA, is awarded the Gutenberg Prize in Mainz for his invention of e-ink and e-paper (the basis of the E-reader).

2001 Hewlett-Packard takes over the company Indigo and systematically expands its liquid-toner technology.

2006 Anilox inking units now also work in sheetfed offset presses.

2008 The PDF is standardised as an open-format ISO 32000. The Prosper inkjet technology introduced by Kodak allows the printing of paper in rolls, with Prosper units also capable of being installed as imprint devices in offset presses. The firm Fujifilm unveils the first inkjet sheetfed press in B2 format. Ryobi introduces the LED UV drying process in offset printing.

2012 Koenig & Bauer introduce the RotaJET inkjet rotation press. The thermal inkjet printer developed by Hewlett-Packard is used for book production. Landa launches the first Nanographic

Printing press, based on inkjet technology with nanometer-sized pigments (at the beta test stage at the time of writing). UV drying becomes more widespread for offset, flexo and digital printing.

2015 Koenig & Bauer's RotaJET is deployed in book production.

2016 Heidelberger Druckmaschinen introduces the Primefire inkjet sheetfed press in B1 format.

2019 Inkjet technology continues to play an increasingly important role in digital printing.

Bibliography

Abbreviations

GJ *Gutenberg-Jahrbuch*, ed. by Stephan Füssel, Mainz,
   Gutenberg-Gesellschaft
GW *Gesamtkatalog der Wiegendrucke* ('Complete Catalogue
   of Incunabula'), ed. by the Commission for the Complete
   Catalogue of Incunabula 1925–40, 2nd revised edn,
   Stuttgart, 1978 ff. Online version, URL: http://www.
   gesamtkatalogderwiegendrucke.de

1. Source material

MANUSCRIPTS AND EARLY PRINTED WORKS
***Göttingen, Germany: Niedersächsische Staats- und
Universitätsbibliothek (SUB)***
Biblia Latina (Gutenberg Bible), Mainz, *c.* 1454 [GW 4201], Shelf
   mark: 2° Bibl. I, 5955: 1, 2 Inc. Rar. Cim
Göttingen Model Book, MS on vellum, *c.* 1450, 8° Cod. MS. Uff. 51
   Cim
Das Helmaspergersche Notariatsinstrument, MS on vellum, Mainz,
   6 November 1455, 2° Cod. MS. hist. lit. 123 Cim
Biblia Latina (with 48 lines), workshop of Johannes Fust and Peter
   Schöffer, Mainz, 1462 [GW 4204], 2° Bibl. I 6002 Inc. Rara
Balbus, Johannes: *Catholicon*, Mainz, *c.* 1460 [GW 3182], 2° Ling.
   IV, 3344 Inc. Rara

Chappe, Paulinus: *Ablassbrief zugunsten der Kirche auf Zypern*, 1455 [GW 6556], 2° Hist. lit. libr. I 751, no. 10

Mainz, Germany: Wissenschaftliche Stadtbibliothek
Biblia Latina, MS on vellum, octavo, 438 fol., Paris revision, possibly northern Italian, third quarter of 13th century, Hs I 38
Biblia Latina, MS, only OT from the Capuchin Library, Mainz, bound *c.* 1455, Hs II 61
Biblia Latina, MS, complete OT and NT in Paris arrangement, octavo, possibly northern France, 650 fol., vellum (so-called Olandus-Bibel), Hs II 67. URN: nbn:de: 0128-3-878
Missale, the so-called 'Gangolph-Missale', MS, *c.* 1444, Hs II 136
Pantaleon, Heinrich: *Prosopographia heroum atque illustrium virorum totius Germaniae*, Basle, 1565, 565 q 2

Paris: Bibliothèque Nationale
Biblia Latina (Gutenberg Bible), copy on vellum, Mainz, *c.* 1454 [GW 4201], Velin 67–70

Washington, DC: Library of Congress
Giant Bible, MS, Mainz, written 4 April 1452–9 July 1453

Würzburg, Germany: Staatsarchiv
'Ernennungsurkunde Gutenbergs zum Hofmann des Erzbischofs 1465'. In: *Mainzer Ingrossaturbücher* 30, Bl. 172
'Bestätigung des Dr Konrad Humery, nach Gutenbergs Tod aus seinem Nachlass die Druckerpresse zurück erhalten zu haben, 26 February 1468'. In: *Erzstift Mainz, Urkunden, Weltlicher Schrank* L 77/79.37

PRINTED SOURCES AND FACSIMILE EDITIONS

The Gutenberg Bible of 1454, facsimile of the copy in the
  Göttingen State and University Library, ed. with commentary
  by Stephan Füssel, 3 vols, Cologne, 2018
Biblia de Gutenberg, facsimile of the copy in the Biblioteca Pública
  del Estado, Burgos, 2 vols, Valencia, 1995
The Göttingen Model Book, facsimile and tr. Hellmut Lehmann-
  Haupt, Columbia, 1972 (2nd edn)
*Johannes Gutenbergs zweiundvierzigzeilige Bibel. Faksimile-Ausgabe
  nach dem Exemplar der Staatsbibliothek Preußischer Kulturbesitz
  Berlin*, Inc. 1511 2°, ed. by Wieland Schmidt and Friedrich Adolf
  Schmidt-Künsemüller, Munich, 1979
Köhler, Johann David: *Hochverdiente und aus bewährten
  Urkunden wohlbeglaubte Ehren-Rettung Johann Gutenbergs* [...],
  Leipzig, 1741
Koelhoff, Johann the Younger: *Die Cronica van der hilliger Stat
  Coellen* (1499), facsimile of the copy in the Diocesan Library,
  Cologne, commentary by Severin Corsten, Hamburg, 1982
Eyn manung der christenheit widder die durken, Mainz
  1454 (facsimile of the sole known copy in the Bayerische
  Staatsbibliothek, Munich), ed. by Ferdinand Geldner,
  Wiesbaden, 1975
Der Mainzer Psalter von 1457, facsimile with commentary, ed. by
  Otto Mazal, Zürich, 1969
Schorbach, Karl: 'Die urkundlichen Nachrichten über Johann
  Gutenberg'. In: *Festschrift zum fünfhundertjährigen Geburtstage
  von Johann Gutenberg*, ed. by Otto Hartwig, Mainz, 1900, pp.
  133–256
Thevet, André: *Le Vrais pourtraits et vies des hommes illustres*, I.
  Keruert & G. Chaudiere, Paris, 1584

2. Bibliography/Research papers

Corsten, Severin, Reinmar Fuchs with the assistance of
Kurt Hans Staub: *Der Buchdruck im 15. Jahrhundert. Eine
Bibliographie*, 2 vols, Stuttgart, 1988/89

Füssel, Stephan: '100 Jahre Gutenberg-Forschung'. In: *Gutenberg-
Festschrift 2000*, Mainz, 2000, pp. 9–26 (GJ, vol. 75)

3. Early printing culture in Asia

*Korea's Early Printing Culture: Seoul 1993 International Symposium
on the Printing History in East and West*, ed. by the Korean
National Commission for Unesco, Seoul, 1997

Füssel, Stephan: *Gutenberg und seine Wirkung. Koreanische
Ausgabe*, Seoul, 2014

Park, Seon Re: 'Six Perspectives in the History of Printing'. In: GJ
1998, pp. 42–7

Park Moon-Year: 'A Study on the Type Casting, Setting and
Printing Method of "Buljo-Jikji-Simche-Voyeol"'. In: GJ 2004,
pp. 32–46

4. Gutenberg

Bechtel, Guy: *Gutenberg et l'invention de l'imprimerie: Une
enquête*, Paris, 1992

Beck, Ulrike: *Hörbuch Johannes Gutenberg. Der Siegeszug des
Buches*, Wissenschaftliche Beratung: Stephan Füssel, Cologne,
2016

Empell, Hans-Michael: *Gutenberg vor Gericht. Der Mainzer
Prozess um die erste gedruckte Bibel*, Frankfurt am Main, 2008 (=
Rechtshistorische Reihe 372)

Füssel, Stephan: *Gutenberg: Il Mondo Cambiato*, Milan, 2001

Füssel, Stephan: *Gutenberg and the Impact of Printing*, tr. by
Douglas Martin, Aldershot, 2005

Füssel, Stephan: *Festschrift zum 550. Todestag Johannes Gutenbergs*
(= GJ 2018), Mainz, 2018

Gutenberg – aventur und kunst. Vom Geheimunternehmen zur ersten Medienrevolution. Katalog zur Ausstellung 2000, Red. Wolfgang Dobras, Mainz, 2000

Johannes Gutenberg – Regionale Aspekte des frühen Buchdrucks. Vorträge der Internationalen Konferenz zum 550. Jubiläum der Buchdruckerkunst 1990 in Berlin, Berlin, 1993 (Beiträge aus der Staatsbibliothek zu Berlin, vol. 1)

Kapr, Albert: *Johannes Gutenberg: The Man and His Invention*, Aldershot, 1996

Lehmann-Haupt, Hellmut: *Gutenberg and the Master of the Playing Cards*, New Haven/London, 1966

Martin, Otto: 'Johannes Gutenberg im Bildnis'. In: *Imprimatur*, new series, vol. XIV, 1991, pp. 109–21

Nemirovskij, Evgenij L.: *Gutenberg und der älteste Buchdruck in Selbstzeugnissen. Chrestomathie und Bibliographie 1454–1550*, Baden-Baden, 2003

Ochs, Heidrun: *Gutenberg und sine frunde. Studien zu patrizischen Familien im spätmittelalterlichen Mainz*, Stuttgart, 2014 (= Geschichtliche Landeskunde 71)

Painter, George D.: 'The Untrue Portraits of Johann Gutenberg'. In: GJ 1967, pp. 54–60

Reske, Christoph: 'Johannes Gutenberg'. In: *Mainz. Eine Stadtgeschichte*, ed. by Franz Dumont and Ferdinand Scherf, Mainz, 2010, pp. 74–8

Reske, Christoph: 'Hat Johannes Gutenberg das Gießinstrument erfunden? Mikroskopischer Typenvergleich an frühen Drucken'. In: GJ 2015, pp. 44–63

Ruppel, Aloys: *Johannes Gutenberg. Sein Leben und Werk*, Berlin, 1939; 2nd edn, Berlin, 1947; reprint Nieuwkoop 1967

Ruppel, Aloys: *Gutenbergs Tod und Begräbnis*, Mainz, 1968 (Kleiner Druck der Gutenberg-Gesellschaft No. 81)

5. The Gutenberg Bible

Davies, Martin: *The Gutenberg Bible*, San Francisco, 1996

Dolgodrova, Tatiana: 'Die Miniaturen der Leipziger Pergament-Ausgabe der Gutenberg-Bibel – zur Zeit in der russischen Staatsbibliothek, Moskau'. In: GJ 97, pp. 64–75

Füssel, Stephan: 'Gutenberg Bible'. In: *Encyclopedia of the Bible and Its Reception*, ed. Dale C. Allison, Berlin, 2015, vol. 10, pp. 1022–4

Füssel, Stephan: *The Gutenberg Bible of 1454*. Facsimile edition of the copy in the Göttingen State and University Library. With a Commentary on the Life and Work of Johannes Gutenberg, the Printing of the Bible, the Distinctive Features of the Göttingen Copy, the *Göttingen Model Book* and the 'Helmasperger Notarial Instrument' by Stephan Füssel, 3 vols, Cologne, 2018 (with co-editions in German, French and Spanish)

Hoffmann, Leonhard: 'Die Gutenbergbibel. Eine Kosten- und Gewinnschätzung des ersten Bibeldrucks auf der Grundlage zeitgenössischer Quellen'. In: *Archiv für Geschichte des Buchwesens* 39, 1993, pp. 255–319

Ing, Janet: *Johann Gutenberg and his Bible: A Historical Study*, New York, 1990

Jensen, Kristian: 'Printing the Bible in the 15th Century. Devotion, Philology and Commerce'. In: *Incunabula and Their Readers: Printing, Selling and Using books in the 15th Century*, ed. by Kristian Jensen, London, 2003

König, Eberhard: *Die Berliner Gutenberg-Bibel*, Darmstadt, 2018

Meuthen, Erich: 'Ein neues frühes Quellenzeugnis (zu Oktober 1454?) für den ältesten Buchdruck. Enea Silvio Piccolomini am 12. März 1455 aus Wiener Neustadt an Kardinal Juan de Carvajal'. In: GJ 1982, pp. 108–18

Miner, Dorothy: *The Giant Bible of Mainz*, Washington, 1952

Needham, Paul: 'The Paper Supply of the Gutenberg Bible'. In: *Papers of the Bibliographical Society of America* 79, 1985, pp. 304–426

Powitz, Gerhardt: *Die Frankfurter Gutenberg-Bibel. Ein Beitrag zum Buchwesen des 15. Jahrhunderts*, Frankfurt am Main, 1990 (Frankfurter Bibliotheksschriften 3)

Schneider, Heinrich: *Der Text der Gutenberg-Bibel zu ihrem 500. Jubiläum untersucht*, Bonn, 1954 (Bonner biblische Beiträge 7)

White, Eric Marshall: *Editio Princeps: A History of the Gutenberg Bible*, London/Turnhout, 2017

6. Individual works by Gutenberg and his immediate contemporaries

'Catholicon-Forschung'. In: *Wolfenbütteler Notizen zur Buchgeschichte* 13, 1988, pp. 105–232

Geldner, Ferdinand: *Der Türkenkalender. Faksimile und Kommentar*, Wiesbaden, 1975

Hellinga, Lotte: 'Das Mainzer *Catholicon* und Gutenbergs Nachlaß. Neudatierung und Auswirkungen'. In: *Archiv für Geschichte des Buchwesens* 40, 1993, pp. 395–416

Hellinga, Lotte: 'Peter Schoeffer and the Book Trade in Mainz: Evidence for the Organisation'. In: *Bookbindings and Other Bibliophily*, ed. by Dennis E. Rhodes, Verona, 1994, pp. 131–83

Hellinga, Lotte: 'Peter Schoeffer and His Organisation: A Bibliographical Investigation of the Ways an Early Printer Worked'. In: *Biblis*, the George Svensson Lectures 1995–6, Stockholm, 1997, pp. 67–106

Schanze, Frieder: 'Wieder einmal das Fragment vom Weltgericht – Bemerkungen und Materialien zur Sybillenweissagung'. In: *Gutenberg-Festschrift 2000*, Mainz, 2000, pp. 42–63

Zedler, Gottfried: *Die Mainzer Ablaßbriefe der Jahre 1454 und 1455*, Mainz, 1913

7. The book and society in the 15th century

Brandis, Thilo: 'Die Handschrift zwischen Mittelalter und Neuzeit. Versuch einer Typologie'. In: GJ 1997, pp. 27–57

Burger, Konrad: *Buchhändleranzeigen des 15. Jahrhunderts*, Leipzig, 1907

Burke, Peter: *A Social History of Knowledge: From Gutenberg to Diderot*, based on the first series of Vonhoff lectures given at the University of Groningen (Netherlands), Cambridge, 2000 (new edition 2004)

Chartier, Roger: *The Cultures of Print: Power and Uses of Print in Modern Europe*, Cambridge, 1989

Eisenstein, Elisabeth L.: *The Printing Press as an Agent of Change*, Cambridge, 1979

Eisermann, Falk and Volker Honemann: 'Die ersten typographischen Einblattdrucke'. In: *Gutenberg-Festschrift 2000*, Mainz, 2000, pp. 88–131

Eisermann, Falk: *Verzeichnis der typographischen Einblattdrucke des 15. Jahrhunderts im Heiligen Römischen Reich Deutscher Nation*, (= VE 15), 3 vols, Wiesbaden, 2004

Febvre, Lucien and Henri-Jean Martin: *The Coming of the Book*, London, 1976

Flasch, Kurt: 'Ideen und Medien. Oder: Gehört Gutenberg in die Geschichte der Philosophie?' In: *Gutenberg-Festschrift 2000*, Mainz, 2000, pp. 27–41

Fleischmann, Isa: *Metallschnitt und Teigdruck. Technik und Entstehung zur Zeit des frühen Buchdrucks*, Mainz, 1998

Füssel, Stephan (ed.): *500 Jahre Schedelsche Weltchronik*, Nuremberg, 1994 (Pirckheimer-Jahrbuch 1994)

Füssel, Stephan and Volker Honemann (eds): *Humanismus und früher Buchdruck*, Nürnberg, 1997 (Pirckheimer-Jahrbuch 1996)

Füssel, Stephan: 'Gutenberg and the Advent of Printing in Western Culture'. In: *Hyphen. A Typographic Forum*, issue 2, vol. 1, Thessaloniki, 1998, pp. 70–6.

Füssel, Stephan: 'Gutenberg and Today's Media Change'. In: *Publishing Research Quarterly* 16, 2001, 4, pp. 4–16

Füssel, Stephan: 'Bible Production in Medieval Monasteries'. In: *In the Beginning was the Word: The Power and Glory of Illuminated Bibles*, ed. by Andreas Fingernagel and Christian Gastgeber, Cologne/London/Los Angeles, 2003, pp. 12–25

Füssel, Stephan: 'Early Modern German Printing'. In: *Early Modern German Literature 1350–1700*, ed. by Max Reinhard, Rochester, NY, 2007, pp. 217–46.

Füssel, Stephan: 'Die Ausbreitung des Buchdrucks in Deutschland und durch deutsche Drucker in Europa (1454–70)'. In: Santoro, Mario (ed.): *Mobilitá dei Mestieri del Libro: Atti del Convegno Roma 2012*, Rome, 2013, pp. 55–75

Füssel, Stephan: 'La Diffusione dell'Arte della Stampa in Europa'. In: *Zwischen Sprachen und Kulturen. Festschrift für Italo Michele Battafarano*, ed. by Elmar Locher, Würzburg, 2016, pp. 235–46

Füssel, Stephan: 'Lucas Cranach the Elder'. In: *The Oxford Encyclopedia of the Bible and the Arts*, ed. by Timothy Beal, Oxford, 2016

Geldner, Ferdinand: *Die deutschen Inkunabeldrucker*, 2 vols, Stuttgart 1968/70

Gier, Helmut and Johannes Janota: *Augsburger Buchdruck und Verlagswesen*, Wiesbaden, 1997

Grafton, Anthony T: 'The Importance of Being Printed'. In: *Journal of Interdisciplinary History* XI, 2, 1980, pp. 265–86

Gumbrecht, Hans Ulrich and K. Ludwig Pfeiffer (eds): *Materialität der Kommunikation*, Frankfurt am Main, 1988

Hall, Edwin: *Sweynheim and Pannartz and the Origins of Printing in Italy: German Technology and Italian Humanism in Renaissance Rome.* McMinville, Oregon, 1991

Harms, Wolfgang and Michael Schilling: *Das illustrierte Flugblatt der frühen Neuzeit*, Stuttgart, 2008

Häussermann, Sabine: *Die Bamberger Pfisterdrucke. Frühe Inkunabelillustration und Medienwandel*, Berlin, 2008 (= Neue Forschungen zur deutschen Kunst 9)

Hellinga, Lotte and J.B.: Trapp (eds): *The Cambridge History of the Book in Britain, Vol. III (1400–1577)*, Cambridge, 1999

Hirsch, Rudolf: *Printing, Selling and Reading 1450–1550*, Wiesbaden, 1974

Honemann, Volker et al. (eds): *Einblattdrucke des 15. und frühen 16. Jahrhunderts. Probleme, Perspektiven, Fallstudien*, Tübingen, 2000

Köhler, Hans-Joachim (ed.): *Flugschriften als Massenmedien der Reformationszeit*, Stuttgart, 1981 (Spätmittelalter und frühe Neuzeit 13)

Krafft, Fritz and Dieter Wuttke (eds): *Das Verhältnis der Humanisten zum Buch*, Boppard, 1977

Kunze, Horst: *Geschichte der Buchillustration in Deutschland. Das 15. Jahrhundert*, 2 vols, Leipzig, 1975

Lowry, Martin: *The World of Aldus Manutius: Business and Scholarship in Renaissance Venice*, Ithaca, 1979

Neddermeyer, Uwe: *Von der Handschrift zum gedruckten Buch*, Wiesbaden, 1998

Schmitz, Wolfgang: *Grundriss der Inkunabelkunde*, Stuttgart, 2018.

Tiemann, Barbara (ed.): *Die Buchkultur im 15. und 16. Jahrhundert*, 2 Halbbände, Hamburg, 1995/99

Wagner, Bettina (ed.): *Xylographa Bavarica. Blockbücher in bayerischen Sammlungen (Xylo-Bav)*, Wiesbaden, 2016 (= Schriftenreihe der Bayerischen Staatsbibliothek 6)

Widmann, Hans: *Der deutsche Buchhandel in Urkunden und Quellen*, Hamburg, 1965

Widmann, Hans: *Vom Nutzen und Nachteil der Erfindung des Buchdrucks – aus der Sicht der Zeitgenossen des Erfinders*, Mainz, 1973 (Kleiner Druck der Gutenberg-Gesellschaft 92)

8. Videos about Gutenberg

The following English-language videos are available on the YouTube channel of the Johannes Gutenberg University, Mainz.

http://www.uni-mainz.de/video/gutenberg/eng/playlist
www.uni-mainz.de/video/gutenberg/eng/00_trailer
www.uni-mainz.de/video/gutenberg/eng/01_metallic_type
www.uni-mainz.de/video/gutenberg/eng/02_manual_typesetting
www.uni-mainz.de/video/gutenberg/eng/03_gutenberg_printing_
press
www.uni-mainz.de/video/gutenberg/eng/04_gutenberg_bible
www.uni-mainz.de/video/gutenberg/eng/05_goettingen_model_
book
www.uni-mainz.de/video/gutenberg/eng/06_dissemination_of_
printing
www.uni-mainz.de/video/gutenberg/eng/07_metallic_type_
mechanization
www.uni-mainz.de/video/gutenberg/eng/08_printing_places
http://www.uni-mainz.de/video/gutenberg/eng/08_printing_
places

Index of names

Conrad III, Archbishop of
Mainz, 17
Crantz, Martin, 100
Cremer, Heinrich, 39

D

Danhauser, Peter, 148
Diether of Isenburg, 75
Dietrich of Erbach, 75
Donatus, Aelius, 15, 61, 63,
78, 112
Dritzehn, Andreas, 19–21
Dünne, Hans, 22
Durand, Guillaume, 49, 70, 89
Dürer, Albrecht, 118

E

Eck, Johannes, 126
Eggestein, Heinrich, 112, 117
Empell, Hans-Michael, 41
Emser, Hieronymus, 126
Erasmus of Rotterdam, 108
Eschenbach, Wolfram von, 95
Etzlaub, Erhard, 127, 129
Euclid, 98

F

Fichet, Guillaume, 100, 146
Frederick III, German
Emperor, 44–45, 133
Freiermut, Hans Heinrich, 126
Friburger, Michael, 100
Froben, Johann, 110

Fust, Christine, 85, 90
Fust, Johannes, 25, 40–42, 49,
75, 85, 87, 90

G

Galen (Ancient Greek
physician), 115,
Gehring, Ulrich, 100
Gelthus, Adam, 79
Gelthus, Arnold (relative), 25,
40
Gelthus, Ort (cousin), 18
Gensfleisch, Friele (brother), 16
Gensfleisch zur Laden,
Friedrich 'Friele' (father),
14, 16
Georg I of Schaumburg, 69
George III, King of England,
89
Gerson, Jean, 5
Ginsheym, Petrus *see* Schöffer,
Peter
Glanville, Bartholomew de, 103
Glockendon, Albrecht, 127
Goethe, Johann Wolfgang von,
151
Grüninger, Johannes, 111
Gunther, Heinrich, 43

H

Heilmann, Andreas, 20–22
Heilmann, Anton, 20
Heilmann, Nikolaus, 22

About the author

Professor Stephan Füssel (b. 1952) was awarded a doctorate by the University of Göttingen in 1983 for his thesis on the literary and cultural ties between Italy and Germany during the Renaissance. In 1991 he gained his postdoctoral qualification at the University of Regensburg with a history of the publishing house established by the leading publisher of the German classical period, Georg Joachim Göschen (1752–1828). Since 1992 Professor Füssel has held the Gutenberg Chair of the University of Mainz at the Gutenberg Institute for World Literature and Written Media and has been Head of the Institute for Book Studies. From 2008 to 2014 he was spokesperson for the University of Mainz's research group on Media Convergence, and from 2002 to 2012 he occupied the post of Director of the Society for the History of Authorship, Reading and Publishing (SHARP). Professor Füssel is also Vice-President of the Willibald Pirckheimer Society for the Study of the Renaissance and Humanism (Nuremberg), an ordinary member of the Historical Commission of the German Publishers and Booksellers Association (Frankfurt am Main) and Vice-President of the International Gutenberg Society (Mainz). He is also editor of the Gutenberg Yearbook, Mainz Studies in Book Studies and the book/e-book series 'Media Convergence'.

Acknowledgments

I should like to thank all the museums and libraries that were involved in supplying the original illustrations reproduced in this book, especially the Göttingen State and University Library (Martin Liebetruth and Dr. Helmut Rohlfing). My thanks are also due to Daniela Füssel and Dr. Christoph Reske for the editorial help they provided.

Picture credits

Gutenberg Museum, Mainz: cover image, 1 and 8, 15, 24, 28, 32
   (photo credit: Martina Pipprich), 62, 77, 79, 82, 83, 86, 119, back
   cover image
John Rylands Library, Manchester: 6
Cheongju Early Printing Museum, Cheongju-si / Korea: 9
Mainz City Archive: 13
Erfurt City Archive (1-1/X B XIII–46): 16
Institute for Book Studies, University of Mainz: 19, 29, 30, 78, 80
   (photo credit: J. Schmidt), 137 (photo credit: Stephan Füssel)
Library of Congress, Washington D. C.: 35
Göttingen State and University Library: 37, 38, 42, 49, 52, 53, 56, 71,
   94, 96, 97, 101, 109, 113, 114, 122
Biblioteca Publica, Burgos: 48
Bavarian State Library, Munich: 58
Herzog August Library, Wolfenbüttel: 68 (Bibel-S. 2° 154), 67 (16.1
   Eth. 2° [1]), 99 (Bibel-S. 2° 151)
Stephan Füssel (photo credit): 73
Leipzig University Library: 90, 91
Germanisches Nationalmuseum, Nuremberg: 125, 128, 130